QUICK QUILTS LARGE AND SMALL

QUICK QUILTS
Large
and
Small

edited by Rosemary Wilkinson

NEW
HOLLAND

First published in 2005 by
New Holland Publishers (UK) Ltd
London ● Cape Town ● Sydney ● Auckland
www.newhollandpublishers.com

Garfield House, 86-88 Edgware Road, London W2 2EA

80 McKenzie Street, Cape Town 8001, South Africa

Unit 4, 14 Aquatic Drive, Frenchs Forest, NSW 2086, Australia

218 Lake Road, Northcote, Auckland, New Zealand

2 4 6 8 10 9 7 5 3 1

ISBN 1 84537 076 7

Editor: Rosemary Wilkinson
Design: Frances de Rees
Photographs: Shona Wood
Illustrations: Carrie Hill
Template diagrams: Stephen Dew

Reproduction by Pica Digital PTE Ltd, Singapore
Printed and bound in Malaysia by
Times Offset (M) Sdn Bhd

NOTE
The measurements for each project are given in imperial and metric. Use only one set of measurements
– do not interchange them because they are not direct equivalents.

Contents

Basic Tools and Techniques

MATERIALS

PATCHWORK FABRICS

The easiest fabrics to work with for patchwork are closely woven, 100% cotton. They "cling" together making a stable unit for cutting and stitching, they don't fray too readily and they press well. Quilting shops and suppliers stock a fantastic range in both solid colours and prints, usually in 45 in/115 cm widths, and most of the quilts in this book are based on these cottons.

BACKING AND BINDING FABRICS

The backing and binding fabrics should be the same type and weight as the fabrics used in the patchwork top. They can be a coordinating colour or a strong contrast. You could also be adventurous and piece the backing, too, to make a reversible quilt. In either case, the colour of the binding needs to work with both the top and the backing fabric designs.

WADDING

Various types of wadding are available in cotton, polyester, wool or mixed fibres. They can be bought in pre-cut sizes suitable for cot quilts and different sizes of bed quilts or in specific lengths cut from a bolt. They also come in different weights or "lofts" depending on how padded you want the quilt to be. Lightweight polyester wadding is the most commonly used, but some wool or cotton types are more suited to hand quilting. Some need to be closely quilted to prevent them from bunching up; others can be quilted up to 8 in/20 cm apart. Follow the manufacturer's instructions if in doubt.

QUANTITIES

The quantities given at the beginning of each project have been calculated to allow for a bit extra – just in case! A few of the quilts combine cutting down the length of the fabric with cutting across the width. This is to make the most economical use of fabric or to obtain border pieces cut in one piece.

Unless otherwise stated, any 10 in/25 cm requirement is the "long" quarter – the full width of the fabric – and not the "fat" quarter, which is a piece 18 x 22 in/50 x 56 cm.

PREPARATION

All fabrics should be washed prior to use in order to wash out any excess dye and to avoid fabrics shrinking at different rates. Wash each fabric separately and rinse – repeatedly if necessary – until the water is clear of any colour run. (If washing in a machine, cut a piece of white fabric from a larger piece. Place one piece in with the wash. After the wash, compare the white fabric with its other half. If they are the same, the fabric did not

run. If a particular fabric continues to colour the water no matter how many times it is washed/rinsed and you have your heart set on using it, try washing it together with a small piece of each of the fabrics you intend to use with it. If these fabrics retain their original colours, i.e. they match the pieces not washed with the offending fabric, you would probably be safe in using it. But if in doubt – don't!

Once washed and before they are completely dry, iron the fabrics and fold them selvage to selvage – as they were originally on the bolt – in preparation for cutting. Be sure to fold them straight so that the selvages line up evenly, even if the cut edges are not parallel (this will be fixed later).

THREADS

For machine quilting use lightweight or monofilament threads. For quilting by hand, use a thread labelled "quilting thread", which is heavier than normal sewing thread. Some threads are 100% cotton; others have a polyester core that is wrapped with cotton. You can use a thread either to match or to contrast with the fabric that is being quilted. Alternatively, use a variegated thread toning or contrasting with the patchwork. It is also acceptable to use several colours on the same piece of work. If the quilt is to be tied rather than quilted, use a heavier thread, such as coton perlé, coton à broder or stranded embroidery cotton.

EQUIPMENT

There are some essential pieces of equipment that have revolutionized the making of patchwork quilts. Rotary cutting equipment, consisting of a rotary cutter used with an acrylic ruler and self-healing cutting mat, has speeded up the process of cutting shapes and made it more accurate; the sewing machine makes assembling the patchwork and quilting the finished piece quick and easy.

SEWING MACHINES

Evermore sophisticated, computerized machines are now available, but even a machine with just a straight stitch will speed up the process of assembling and quilting the patchwork considerably. Most sewing machines have a swing needle that allows the zig-zag stitching used for securing appliqué patches. Machines with decorative stitches provide the opportunity for additional embellishments, as in the Love and Kisses quilt.

LONGARM QUILTING MACHINES

These machines are used by professional quilters. You can choose from a huge library of quilting designs. There is also the option to have edge-to-edge quilting, all-over quilting of one design over the entire quilt, or a combination of patterns to complement each other. Alternatively, you can specify your own freehand style.

One of the advantages of this machine is that the quilt sandwich does not need to be tacked or pinned together prior to quilting: the pieced top, wadding and backing are mounted onto separate rollers that are part of the frame of the machine.

The machine is hand operated and takes considerable skill to work successfully. Most of the quilters who offer this quilting service advertize in patchwork magazines.

ROTARY CUTTING

Rotary cutting has become the most commonly used method of cutting fabrics for patchwork. Most rotary cutting tools are available with either imperial or metric measurements.

Rotary Cutters

There are several different makes available, mainly in three different sizes: small, medium and large. The medium size (45 mm) is probably the one most widely used and perhaps the easiest to control. The smallest can be difficult to use with rulers. The largest is very useful when cutting through several layers of fabric but can take some practice to use. The rotary blade is extremely sharp, so be sure to observe the safety instructions given on page 8. It does become blunted with frequent use, so be sure to have replacement blades available.

Rotary Rulers

Various different rulers are available for use with rotary cutters. These are made of acrylic and are sufficiently thick to act as a guide for the rotary blade. You must use these rulers with the rotary cutter. Do not use metal rulers, as they will severely damage the blades.

The rulers are marked with measurements and angled lines used as a guide when cutting the fabrics. Ideally, these markings should be on the underside of the ruler, laser printed and easy to read. Angles should be marked in both directions. Different makes of rulers can have the lines printed in different colours. Choose one that you find easy on your eyes. Some makes also have a non-slip surface on the back – a very helpful addition.

The two most useful basic rulers are either a 24 x 6 in/60 x 15 cm, or one that is slightly shorter, and the small bias square ruler, $6\frac{1}{2}$ in or 15 cm. This ruler is particularly useful for marking squares containing two triangles – the half-square triangle units. There are many other rulers designed for specific jobs that you can purchase if and when needed.

Self-healing Rotary Cutting Mats

These are essential companions to the rotary cutter and ruler. Do not attempt to cut on any other surface. The mats come in a number of different sizes and several different colours. The smaller ones are useful to take to classes, but for use at home, purchase the largest that you can afford and that suits your own workstation. There is usually a grid on one side, although both sides can be used. The lines on the mat are not always accurate, so it's better to use the lines on the ruler if possible.

OTHER USEFUL EQUIPMENT

Most other pieces of equipment are those that you will already have in your workbox. Those listed below are essential, but there is also a vast array of special tools devised by experienced quiltmakers that have specific uses. They are not needed by the beginner quilter but can really enhance the planning, cutting and quilting of your designs.

Scissors: Two pairs are needed. One large pair of good-quality scissors should be used exclusively for cutting fabric. The second, smaller pair is for cutting paper, card or template plastic.

Markers: Quilting designs can either be traced or drawn on the fabric prior to the layering or added after the layering with the aid of stencils or templates. Various marking tools are available: 2H pencils; silver, yellow or white pencils; fade away or washable marking pens; and Hera markers (which lightly indent the fabric). Whatever your choice, test the markers on a scrap of the fabric used in the quilt to ensure that the marks can be removed.

Pins: Good-quality, clean, rustproof, straight pins are essential when a pin is required to hold the work in place for piecing. Flat-headed flower pins are useful because they don't add bulk.

Safety pins: These are useful for holding the quilt "sandwich" together for quilting, especially for those who prefer to machine quilt or want the speed of not tacking/basting the three layers together. Place the pins at regular intervals all over the surface.

Needles: For hand quilting, use "quilting" or "betweens" needles. Most quilters start with a no. 8 or 9 and progress to a no. 10 or 12. For machine stitching, the needles numbered 70/10 or 80/12 are both suitable for piecing and quilting. For tying with thicker thread, use a crewel or embroidery needle.

Thimbles: Two thimbles will be required for hand quilting. One thimble is worn on the hand pushing the needle and the other on the hand underneath the quilt "receiving" the needle. There are various types on the market ranging from metal to plastic to leather sheaths for the finger. There are also little patches that stick to the finger to protect it.

HOOPS AND FRAMES

These are only needed if you are quilting by hand. They hold a section of the quilt under light tension to help you to achieve an even stitch. There are many types and sizes available, ranging from round and oval hoops to standing frames made of plastic pipes and wooden fixed frames.

Hoops are perhaps the easiest for a beginner. The 14 in/ 35 cm or 16 in/40 cm are best for portability. Many quilters continue to use hoops in preference to standing frames. When the quilt is in the hoop, the surface of the quilt should not be taut, as is the case with embroidery. If you place the quilt top with its hoop on a table, you should be able to push the fabric in the centre of the hoop with your finger and touch the table beneath. Without this "give", you will not be able to "rock" the needle for the quilting stitch. Do not leave the quilt in a hoop when you are not working on it, as the hoop will distort the fabrics.

TECHNIQUES

ROTARY CUTTING

The basis of rotary cutting is that fabric is cut first in strips – usually across the width of the fabric, then cross-cut into squares or rectangles. Unless otherwise stated, fabric is used folded selvage to selvage, wrong sides together, as it has come off the bolt.

MAKING THE EDGE STRAIGHT

Before any accurate cutting can be done, you must first make sure the cut edge of the fabric is at right angles to the selvages.
1 Place the folded fabric on the cutting mat with the fabric smoothed out, the selvages exactly aligned at the top and the bulk of the fabric on the side that is not your cutting hand. Place the ruler on the fabric next to the cut edge, aligning the horizontal lines on the ruler with the fold and with the selvages.
2 Place your non-cutting hand on the ruler to hold it straight and apply pressure. Keep the hand holding the ruler in line with the cutting hand. Place the cutter on the mat just below the fabric and up against the ruler. Start cutting by running the cutter upwards and right next to the edge of the ruler (diagram 1).

diagram 1

SAFETY

All rotary cutters have some form of safety mechanism that should always be used. Close the safety cover over the blade after every cut you make, whether or not you intend to continue with another cut. Safety habits are essential and will help prevent accidents. Ensure that the cutters are safely stored out of the reach of children.

Keep the cutter clean and free of fluff. An occasional drop of sewing machine oil helps it to rotate smoothly. Avoid running over pins, as this ruins the blade. Renew the blade as soon as it becomes blunt, as a blunt blade makes for inaccurate and difficult cutting and can damage the cutting mat. Replacement blades are readily available and there are also blade sharpening/exchange services.

3 When the cutter becomes level with your extended fingertips, stop cutting but leave the cutter in position and carefully move the hand holding the ruler further along the ruler to keep the applied pressure in the area where the cutting is taking place. Continue cutting and moving the steadying hand as necessary until you have cut completely across the fabric. As soon as the cut is complete, close the safety shield on the cutter. If you run out of cutting mat, you will need to reposition the fabric, but this is not ideal as it can bring the fabric out of alignment.
4 Open out the narrow strip of fabric just cut off. Check to make sure that a "valley" or a "hill" has not appeared at the point of the fold on the edge just cut; it should be perfectly straight. If it is not, the fabric was not folded correctly. Fold the fabric again, making sure that this time the selvages are exactly aligned. Make another cut to straighten the edge and check again.

CUTTING STRIPS

The next stage is to cut strips across the width of the fabric. To do this, change the position of the fabric to the opposite side of the board, then use the measurements on the ruler to cut the strips.
1 Place the fabric on the cutting mat on the side of your cutting hand. Place the ruler on the mat so that it overlaps the fabric. Align the cut edge of the fabric with the vertical line on the ruler that corresponds to the measurement that you wish to cut. The horizontal lines on the ruler should be aligned with the folded edge and the selvage of the fabric.
2 As before, place one hand on the ruler to apply pressure while cutting the fabric with the other hand (diagram 2).

diagram 2

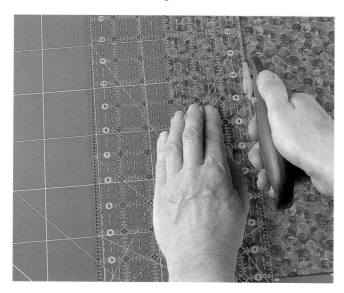

CROSS-CUTTING

The strips can now be cut into smaller units, described as cross-cutting, and these units are sometimes sub-cut into triangles.

Squares

1 Place the strip just cut on the cutting mat with the longest edge horizontal to you and most of the fabric on the side of the non-cutting hand. Cut off the selvages in the same way in which you straightened the fabric edge at the start of the process.

2 Now place the strip on the opposite side of the mat and cut across (cross-cut) the strip using the same measurement on the rule as used for cutting the strip; ensure that the horizontal lines of the ruler align with the horizontal edge of the fabric. You have now created two squares of the required measurement (diagram 3). Repeat as required.

diagram 3

Rectangles

1 First cut a strip to one of the required side measurements for the rectangle. Remove the selvages.
2 Turn the strip to the horizontal position as for the squares.
3 Cross-cut this strip using the other side measurement required for the rectangle. Again, ensure that the horizontal lines of the ruler align with the horizontal cut edges of the strip.

Wide Strips

Placing two rulers side by side can aid the cutting of extra-wide strips. If you don't have two rulers, place the fabric on the cutting mat in the correct position for cutting. Align the cut edge of the fabric with one of the vertical lines running completely across the cutting board, and the folded edge with one of the horizontal lines. If the measurement does not fall on one of the lines on the cutting mat, use the ruler in conjunction with the cutting mat.

Multi-strip Units

This two-stage method of cutting strips, then cross-cutting into squares or rectangles, can also be used to speed up the cutting of multi-strip units to provide strip blocks, such as those used for the Floral Garland quilt.

1 Cut the required number and size of strips and stitch together as per the instructions for the block/quilt you are making. Press the seams and check that they are smooth on the right side of the strip unit with no pleats or wrinkles.

2 Place the unit right side up in the horizontal position on the cutting mat. Align the horizontal lines on the ruler with the longer cut edges of the strips and with the seam lines just created (diagram 4). If, after you have cut a few cross-cuts, the lines on the ruler do not line up with the cut edges as well as the seam lines, re-cut the end to straighten it before cutting any more units.

diagram 4

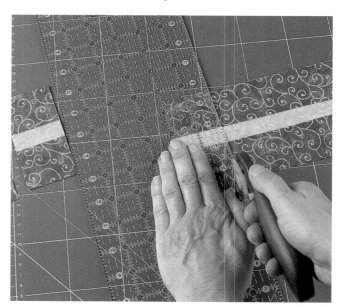

ROTARY CUTTING TRIANGLES

Squares can be divided into either two or four triangles, called half-square or quarter-square triangles. Both sizes of triangle can be quickly cut using the rotary cutter or they can be made even faster by a quick piecing method described on pages 11 and 12.

Cutting Half-square Triangles

1 Cut the fabric into strips of the correct depth and remove the selvages.

2 Cross-cut the strips into squares of the correct width.

3 Align the 45° angle line on the ruler with the sides of the square and place the edge of the ruler so that it goes diagonally across the square from corner to corner. Cut the square on this diagonal, creating two half-square triangles (diagram 5).

diagram 5

Cutting Quarter-square Triangles

1 Cut the fabric into strips of the correct depth and remove the selvages.

2 Cross-cut the strips into squares of the correct width.

3 Cut the square into two half-square triangles, as above.

4 You can either repeat this procedure on the other diagonal (diagram 6) or, if you are wary of the fabric slipping now that it is in two pieces, separate the two triangles and cut them individually. Align one of the horizontal lines of the ruler with the long edge of the triangle, the 45° line with the short edge of the triangle and the edge of the ruler placed on the point of the triangle opposite the long edge. Cut this half-square triangle into two quarter-square triangles.

diagram 6

SEAMS

To stitch accurately, you must be able to use the correct seam allowance without having to mark it on the fabric. To do this, you use the foot or the bed of your sewing machine as a guide. Many machines today have a "$1/4$ in" or "patchwork" foot available as an extra. There are also various generic foot accessories available that will fit most machines. Before you start any piecing, check that you can make this seam allowance accurately.

Checking the Machine for the Correct Seam Allowance

Unthread the machine. Place a piece of paper under the presser foot, so that the right-hand edge of the paper aligns with the right-hand edge of the presser foot. Stitch a seam line on the paper. A row of holes will appear. Remove the paper from the machine and measure the distance from the holes to the edge of the paper. If it is not the correct width, i.e. $1/4$ in/0.75 cm, try one of the following:

1 If your machine has a number of different needle positions, try moving the needle in the direction required to make the seam allowance accurate. Try the test of stitching a row of holes again.

2 Draw a line on the paper to the correct seam allowance, i.e. $1/4$ in/0.75 cm from the edge of the paper. Place the paper under the presser foot, aligning the drawn line with the needle. Lower the presser foot to hold the paper securely and, to double-check, lower the needle to ensure that it is directly on top of the drawn line.

Fix a piece of masking tape on the bed of the machine so that the left-hand edge of the tape lines up with the right-hand edge of the paper. This can also be done with magnetic strips available on the market to be used as seam guides. But do take advice on using these if your machine is computerized or electronic.

Stitching ¼ in/0.75 cm Seams

When stitching pieces together, line up the edge of the fabric with the right-hand edge of the presser foot or with the left-hand edge of the tape or the magnetic strip on the bed of your machine, if you have used this method.

Checking the Fabric for the Correct Seam Allowance

As so much of the success of a patchwork depends on accuracy of cutting and seaming, it is worth double-checking on the fabric that you are stitching a ¼ in/0.75 cm seam.

Cut three strips of fabric 1½ in/4 cm wide. Stitch these together along the long edges. Press the seams away from the centre strip. Measure the centre strip. It should measure exactly 1 in/2.5 cm wide. If not, reposition the needle/tape and try again.

Stitch Length

The stitch length used is normally 12 stitches to the inch or 5 to the centimetre. If the pieces being stitched together are to be cross-cut into smaller units, it is advisable to slightly shorten the stitch, which will mean the seam is less likely to unravel. It is also good practice to start each new project with a new needle in a clean machine – free of fluff around the bobbin housing.

QUICK MACHINE PIECING

The three most basic techniques are for stitching pairs of patches together (chain piecing), for stitching half-square triangle units and for stitching quarter-square triangle units.

Chain Piecing

Have all the pairs of patches or strips together ready in a pile. Place the first two patches or strips in the machine, right sides together, and stitch them together. Just before reaching the end, stop stitching and pick up the next two patches or strips. Place them on the bed of the machine, so that they just touch the patches under the needle. Stitch off one set and onto the next. Repeat this process until all the pairs are stitched to create a "chain" of pieced patches/strips (diagram 7). Cut the thread

diagram 7

between each unit to separate them. Open out and press the seams according to the instructions given with each project.

Stitching Half-square Triangle Units

This is a quick method of creating a bi-coloured square without cutting the triangles first.

1 Cut two squares of different coloured fabrics to the correct measurement, i.e. the finished size of the bi-coloured square plus ⅝ in/1.75 cm. Place them right sides together, aligning all raw edges. On the wrong side of the top square, draw a diagonal line from one corner to the other.

2 Stitch ¼ in/0.75 cm away on either side of the drawn line (diagram 8).

diagram 8

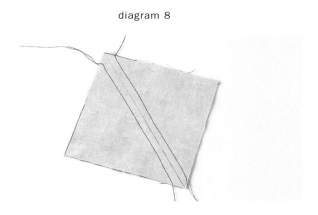

3 Cut the two halves apart by cutting on the drawn line. Open out and press the seams according to the instructions given with each project. You now have two squares, each containing two triangles. Trim off the corners (diagram 9).

diagram 9

Stitching Quarter-square Triangle Units

This method also creates triangles from squares without first cutting the triangles.

1 Cut squares to the finished size of a square containing four triangles plus $1\frac{1}{4}$ in/3.5 cm. Follow the stitching, cutting apart and pressing sequence as for the half-square triangles units.

2 Place the two bi-coloured squares right sides together. Ensure that each triangle is facing a triangle of a different colour. Draw a line diagonally from corner to corner, at right angles to the stitched seam.

3 Pin carefully to match the seams, then stitch $\frac{1}{4}$ in/0.75 cm away on either side of the line. Before cutting apart, open up each side and check to see that the points match in the centre (diagram 10).

diagram 10

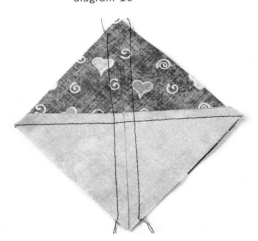

4 Cut apart on the drawn line. You now have two squares, each containing four triangles (diagram 11).

diagram 11

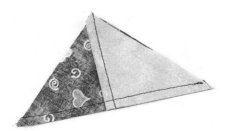

PRESSING

Each project will have instructions on the direction in which to press the seam allowances. These have been designed to facilitate easier piecing at junctions and to reduce the bulk so that seam allowances do not lay one on top of the other. Pressing as you complete each stage of the piecing will also improve the accuracy and look of your work. Take care not to distort the patches. Be gentle, not fierce, with the iron.

ADDING THE BORDERS

Most patchwork tops are framed by one or more borders. The simplest way of adding borders is to add strips first to the top and bottom of the quilt and then to the sides, producing abutted corners. A more complicated method is to add strips to adjacent sides and join them with seams at 45 degrees, giving mitred borders. Only the first method is used for the quilts in this book.

Adding Borders with Abutted Corners

The measurements for the borders required for each quilt in the book will be given in the instructions. However, it is always wise to measure your own work to determine the actual measurement.

1 Measure the quilt through the centre across the width edge to edge. Cut the strips for the top and bottom borders to this length by the width specified for the border.

2 Pin the strips to the quilt by pinning first at each end, then in the middle, then evenly spaced along the edge. By pinning in this manner, it is possible to ensure that the quilt "fits" the border. Stitch the border strips into position on the top and bottom edge of the quilt (diagram 12). Press the seams towards the border.

diagram 12

3 Measure the quilt through the centre from top to bottom. Cut the side border strips to this measurement.
4 Pin and stitch the borders to each side of the quilt as before (diagram 13). Press the seams towards the border.

diagram 13

QUILTING

The three layers or "sandwich" of the backing/wadding/pieced top are held together by quilting or by tying. The quilting can be done by hand or machine. The tying is done by hand stitching decorative ties at strategic points on the quilt. Buttons can also be used for the same purpose.

NOTES

SEAMS

Unless otherwise stated, the seam allowances are included in the measurements given and are always $\frac{1}{4}$ in for imperial and 0.75 cm for metric. The metric seam allowance is slightly bigger than the imperial, but it is easy to use in conjunction with the various rotary cutting rulers on the market.

MEASUREMENTS

The measurements in the quilt instructions are given in both imperial and metric. Use only one set of measurements in any project – do not interchange them, because they are not direct equivalents.

Layering/Sandwiching

Prior to any quilting, unless you are using a longarm quilting machine (see page 6), the pieced top must be layered with the wadding and the backing. The wadding and the backing should be slightly larger than the quilt top – approximately 2 in/5 cm on all sides. There are two different methods for assembling the three layers depending on whether the quilts has bound edges or not.

Assembling Prior to Binding

1 Lay out the backing fabric wrong side uppermost. Ensure that it is stretched out and smooth. Secure the edges with masking tape at intervals along the edges to help to hold it in position.
2 Place the wadding on top of the backing fabric. If you need to join two pieces of wadding first, butt the edges and stitch together by hand using a herringbone stitch (diagram 14).

diagram 14

3 Place the pieced top right side up and centred on top of the wadding.

Assembling Where No Binding is Used – Called "Bagging Out"

1 Spread out the wadding on a flat surface. Smooth out to ensure there are no wrinkles.
2 Place the backing fabric centrally on top of the wadding, right side uppermost.
3 Place the pieced top centrally over the backing, wrong side uppermost. Pin with straight pins around the edges to keep them together.
4 Stitch around all four sides with a $\frac{1}{4}$ in/0.75 cm seam allowance but leaving an opening of about 15–18 in/35–45 cm in one of the sides.
5 Trim the excess wadding and backing at the sides and across the corners to reduce bulk, then turn the quilt right side out, so that the wadding is in the middle. Slip-stitch the opening closed.
6 Smooth out the layers of the quilt and roll and finger-press the edges so that the seam lies along the edge or just underneath.

Basting Prior to Quilting

If the piece is to be quilted rather than tied, the three layers now need to be held together at regular intervals. This can be done by basting or by using safety pins. For either method, start in the centre of the quilt and work out to the edges.

Using a long length of thread, start basting in the centre of the quilt top. Only pull about half of the thread through as you start stitching. Once you have reached the edge, go back and thread the other end of the thread and baste to the opposite edge. Repeat this process, stitching in a grid of horizontal and vertical lines over the whole quilt top (diagram 15).

diagram 15

MACHINE QUILTING

Designs to be used for machine quilting should ideally be those that have one continuous line. The lines can be straight or free-form curves and squiggles. For either type, be sure to keep the density of stitching the same. With either method, continuous lines of stitching will be visible both on the top and on the back of the quilt. It is a quick method but requires careful preparation.

There is a wide variety of tools available designed to help make handling the quilt easier during the machine quilting process. However, the most essential requirement is practice.

It is worth making up a practice sandwich – if possible using the same fabrics and wadding as used in the actual quilt – to be sure that you get the effect you want. In any case, plan the quilting design first, otherwise there is a danger that you will start with quite dense stitching, then tire of the process and begin to space out the lines, producing an uneven pattern.

When starting and stopping the stitching during machine quilting, either reduce the stitch length to zero or stitch several stitches in one spot. If you do not like the build-up of stitches that this method produces, leave long tails on the thread when you start and stop. Later, pull these threads through to one side of the quilt, knot them, then thread them into a needle. Push the needle into the fabric and into the wadding, but not through to the other side of the quilt, and then back out through the fabric again about 1 in/2.5 cm away from where the needle entered the quilt. Cut off the excess thread.

In-the-ditch Machine Quilting

One of the easiest and most common forms of straight line quilting is called "in-the-ditch" and involves stitching just beside a seam line on the side without the seam allowances. Some machines require a walking foot to stitch the three layers together. These are used with the feed dogs up and, while in use, the machine controls the direction and stitch length.

Free Motion Machine Quilting

When machine quilting in freehand, a darning foot is used with the feed dogs down, so that you can move the quilt forwards, backwards and sideways. This is easier on some machines than others, but all require a bit of practice.

Hand Quilting

The stitch used for hand quilting is a running stitch. The needle goes into the quilt through to the back and returns to the top of the quilt all in one movement. The aim is to have the size of the stitches and spaces between them the same.

1 Thread a needle with an 18 in/45 cm length of quilting thread and knot the end. Push the needle into the fabric and into the wadding, but not through to the back, about 1 in/2.5 cm away from where you want to start stitching. Bring the needle up through the fabric at the point where you will begin stitching. Gently pull on the thread to "pop" the knot through into the wadding.

2 To make a perfect quilting stitch, the needle needs to enter the fabric perpendicular to the quilt top. Holding the needle between your first finger and thumb, push the needle into the fabric until it hits the thimble on the finger of the hand underneath.

3 The needle can now be held between the thimble on your sewing hand and the thimble on the finger underneath. Release your thumb and first finger hold on the needle. Place your thumb on the quilt top just in front of where the needle will come back up to the top and gently press down on the quilt (diagram 16).

diagram 16

4 At the same time, rock the thread end of the needle down towards the quilt top and push the needle up from underneath so that the point appears on the top of the quilt. You can either pull the needle through now, making only one stitch, or rock the needle up to the vertical again, push the needle through to the back, then rock the needle up to the quilt top, again placing another stitch on the needle. Repeat until you can no longer rock the needle into a completely upright position (diagram 17). Pull the needle through the quilt. One stitch at a time or several placed on the needle at once – "the rocking stitch" – before pulling the thread through, are both acceptable.

diagram 17

5 When the stitching is complete, tie a knot in the thread close to the quilt surface. Push the needle into the quilt top and the wadding next to the knot, but not through to the back of the quilt. Bring the needle up again about 1 in/2.5 cm away and gently tug on the thread to "pop" the knot through the fabric and into the wadding. Cut the thread.

BINDING

Once the quilting is completed, the quilt is usually (but not always) finished off with a binding to enclose the raw edges. This binding can be cut on the straight or on the bias. Either way, the binding is usually best done with a double fold. It can be applied in four separate pieces to each of the four sides, or the binding strips can be joined together and stitched to the quilt in one continuous strip with mitred corners. To join straight-cut pieces for a continuous strip, use straight seams; to join bias-cut pieces, use diagonal seams (diagram 18).

diagram 18

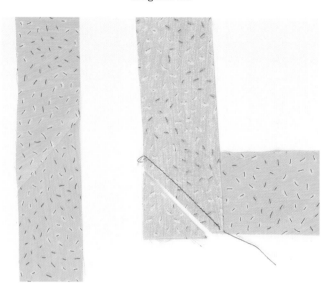

For either method, the width of the bias strips should be cut to the following measurement: finished binding width x four + the seam allowance x two.

For example:
A finished binding width of $^1\!/_2$ in would be cut as $2^1\!/_2$ in:
$(^1\!/_2$ in x 4$) + (^1\!/_4$ in x 2$) = 2^1\!/_2$ in
or 1.25 cm would be cut 6.5 cm:
$(1.25$ cm x 4$) + (0.75$ cm x 2$) = 6.5$ cm

Binding the Four Sides Separately
1 Cut binding strips to the required width. Fold in half lengthwise with wrong sides together and lightly press.
2 Measure the quilt through the centre from top to bottom and cut two of the binding strips to this length.
3 Pin one of the strips down the side of the quilt, right sides together and aligning raw edges. Stitch with the usual seam allowance.
4 Fold the binding strip to the back of the quilt and slip stitch to the backing fabric. Trim the ends level with the wadding. Do the same on the opposite side of the quilt with the other strip.
5 Measure the quilt through the centre from side to side and add

$1\frac{1}{2}$ in/4 cm for turnings. Cut two more binding strips to this length, joining if necessary. Stitch to the top and bottom of the quilt, leaving a $\frac{3}{4}$ in/2 cm overhang at each end. Turn in a short hem at either end before folding to the back and slip-stitching down. Slip-stitch the corners neatly.

Continuous Strip Binding

1 Fold the binding in half lengthwise with wrong sides together and lightly press.

2 Place the raw edges of the binding to the raw edge of the quilt – somewhere along one side, not at a corner. Commence stitching about 1 in/2.5 cm from the end of the binding and, using the specified seam allowance, stitch the binding to the quilt through all layers of the "sandwich" (diagram 19). Stop $\frac{1}{4}$ in/0.75 cm from the end. At this point, backstitch to secure, then break off the threads. Remove the quilt from the sewing machine.

diagram 19

3 Place the quilt on a flat surface, with the binding just stitched at the top edge; fold the binding up and away from the quilt to "twelve o'clock", creating a 45° fold at the corner (diagram 20).

diagram 20

4 Fold the binding back down to "six o'clock" aligning the raw edges of the binding to the raw edge of the quilt. The fold created on the binding at the top should be the same distance away from the seam as the width of the finished binding (diagram 21).

diagram 21

5 Start stitching the binding to the quilt at the same point where the previous stitching stopped. Secure with backstitching, then continue to the next corner. Repeat the process at each corner.

6 Stop about 2 in/5 cm from where you started. Open out the fold on both ends of the binding, then seam the two ends together. Trim away the excess, refold and finish applying the binding to the quilt.

7 Trim the excess wadding and backing fabric so that the distance from the stitching line equals or is slightly wider than that of the finished binding. Fold the binding over to the back and hand stitch the folded edge of the binding to the quilt along the row of machine stitching just created. A mitre will appear at the corners on the front and on the back of the binding. Slip-stitch these in place (diagram 22).

diagram 22

HANGING SLEEVE

If your quilt is a wallhanging or is to be exhibited, it will need a hanging sleeve. A sleeve can be added after the quilt is completely finished, but a more secure and permanent sleeve can be added along with the binding. Stitch the binding to the front of the quilt and, before folding it over onto the back, add the sleeve.

1 Cut a piece of fabric, preferably matching the backing, to measure 10 in/25 cm deep by the width of the quilt. Make a 1 in/ 2.5 cm hem on both the short ends.

2 Fold the fabric in half along the length with wrong sides together. Centre this on the back of the quilt, aligning the raw edges of the sleeve with the raw edges of the quilt. Secure with pins (diagram 23).

diagram 23

3 Turn the quilt over so the front is uppermost. Taking care to remove the pins as you approach them, stitch the sleeve to the quilt by stitching along the row of stitching made when applying the binding.

4 Finish hand stitching on the binding.

5 Lay the quilt on a flat surface with the back uppermost. Smooth out the sleeve and pin the lower edge so that it rests evenly on the back of the quilt and pin (diagram 24).

diagram 24

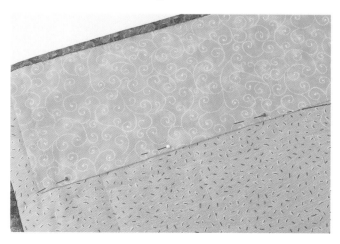

6 Stitch the sleeve to the back of the quilt along the fold at the bottom of the sleeve, then stitch the underneath edge at each short end, so that when a rod is inserted it will not actually touch the back of the quilt, only the sleeve fabric. Take care that your stitches only go into the back and wadding of the quilt and are not visible on the front. Remove the pins.

LABELLING

Your quilt should be signed, dated and placed. This information provides a record for your own information as well as for future admirers.

The details can be incorporated on the quilt front or on a label attached to the back. This label can be simply handwritten with a permanent pen or made very elaborate with pieced, embroidered or fabric painting. Another way of making an individual label is with the help of modern technology: the computer and the colour printer.

HINTS AND TIPS

Chain Piecing

To further speed up this process, place the two pieces/strips to be stitched together beside the sewing machine. Place one group of patches facing up and one group facing down. Now when you pick up one piece, its partner is in the correct position to place on top, right sides together.

Pressing Seams

Always press seams to one side unless otherwise stated, as an open seam is put under more strain. Press fabrics towards the darker fabric to prevent show-through.

Slip-stitched Seams

To finish the slip-stitched seam neatly (e.g. when bagging out a quilt), before you turn your quilt, stitch across the turning opening using the longest stitch your machine will make. Finger-press the seam allowance open quite firmly. Now rip out the long stitches, turn the quilt and you will find you have an obvious straight crease line to follow when hand stitching.

Measuring Borders

Even if measurements are given for border strips, it is always worth double-checking against your own pieced top. Measure through the middle of the quilt, as the edges can become stretched.

Attaching Borders

Once you have determined the size of the top, bottom and side borders, fit the pieced top to these measurements rather than the other way round. Mark the centre and quarter points of the borders and of the quilt sides and match up. You may need to ease the sides of the quilt to fit the borders, but this will help to produce a flat, square quilt rather than one with wavy borders.

Storage

Store quilts in an old pillowcase or acid-free tissue paper rather than in a plastic bag, which doesn't allow fabrics to breathe and therefore encourages mould.

Roman Stripe Crib Quilt

DESIGNED
BY
Alison Wood

For a crib quilt with a difference, I've made the Roman Stripe block, perhaps more often seen in Amish colours, in a clear soft plain blue with accents of soft pink and mauve and a darker blue for depth. Strip piecing and rotary cutting speed up the assembling, and the only points that need to be matched are those between the blocks.

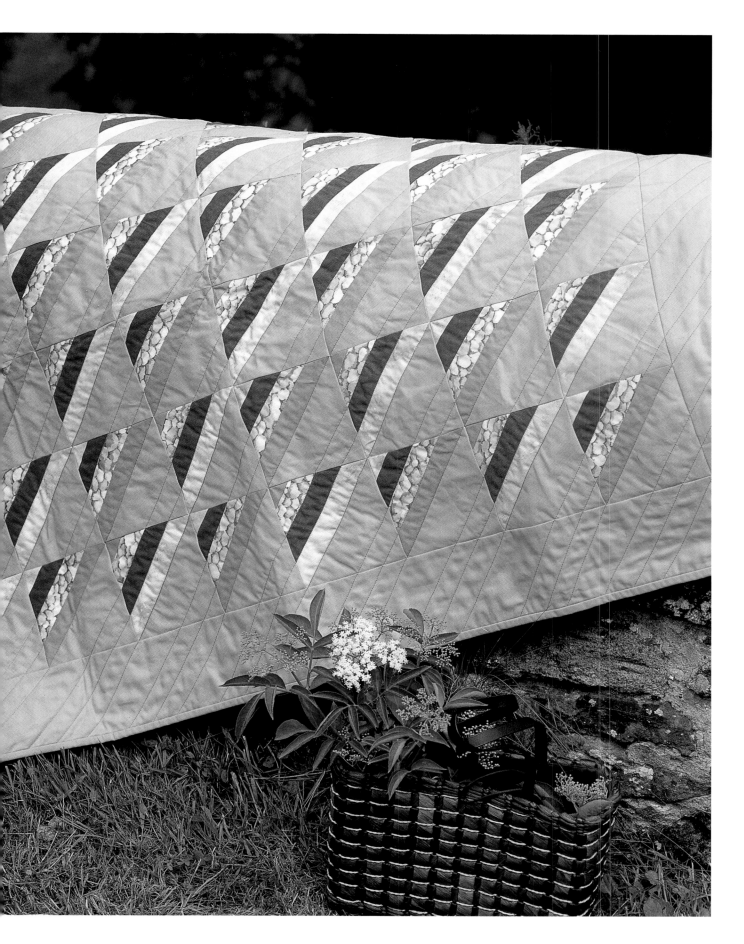

Quilt assembly diagram

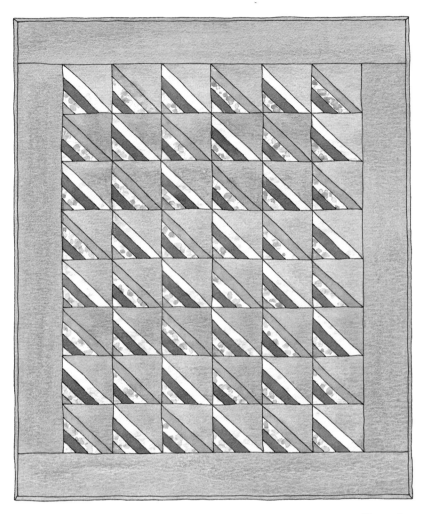

Finished size: 38 x 48 in/96 x 122 cm

Materials

All the fabrics used in the quilt top are 45 in/115 cm wide, 100% cotton

For the blocks: 20 in/50 cm of each of four fabrics for the stripes (I used three pinks and a blue)

For the background, borders and binding: 2 yds/2 m in total (if choosing different fabrics for each of these, allow 1 yd/1 m for background of blocks, 24 in/60 cm for borders and 12 in/40 cm for binding)

Backing: 1½ yds/1.5 m

Wadding: Approximately 45 x 60 in/115 x 150 cm (cot size). Cotton or 80:20 cotton/polyester mix is more suitable for machine quilting. For hand quilting, use either cotton/cotton blend or 2 oz polyester

Cutting

1 From each of the four fabrics chosen for the striped half of the block, cut six strips, 1½ in/4 cm deep, across the width of the fabric.

2 From the border fabric, cut four strips, 4½ in/11.5 cm deep, across the width of the fabric.

3 From the binding fabric, cut four strips, 2½ in/6.5 cm deep, across the width of the fabric.

NOTE

Do not cut the remainder of the background fabric until you have made the strip sets (see page 22).

Alternative colour schemes

1 Traditional Amish plain colours sing out against a black background.

2 A subtle blended effect is achieved with low contrast florals and soft stripes.

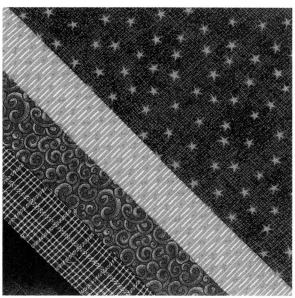

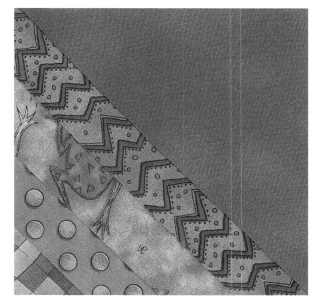

3 A selection of country blues and golds are easy on the eyes.

4 Fun prints in fuchsia pink and electric blue for a stunning effect.

Stitching

1 Make six identical strip sets as follows: lay out the 1½ in/4 cm strips from each of the four colours in the order in which you wish them to appear in the block. Study the quilt assembly diagram on page 20 and you will see that there are two alternate blocks featuring the same fabrics but in reverse order (diagram 1). Both versions need to look good against the background you have chosen. Both will be cut from the same strip set.

diagram 1

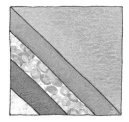 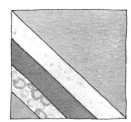

2 Stitch the strips together in the chosen order, right sides together, along the length of the strips, keeping to an accurate ¼ in/0.75 cm seam allowance. Take care not to stretch the strips as you stitch them, as this can lead to bowing and distortion. Alternating the direction of sewing can help to prevent curving. Chain piecing the strips will save time and thread. Be consistent about the direction in which you press your seam allowances.

NOTE

Careful pressing is important for the accuracy of this technique. Press the seams joining the strips flat first; this "sets" the seam, causing the thread to sink into the fabric a little. Then, using the side of the iron, press from the right side to ensure there are no little pleats beside the seams. Press the seam allowances in the same direction. Try to press rather than to iron the fabric, as you do not want to curve the stitched strip set.

3 If you have pre-washed your fabrics or they are only lightly dressed, you may wish at this stage to lightly mist the strip units with spray starch from the right side and

press carefully. The addition of starch will help to stabilize the bias edges, which will be exposed when you cut the strip sets into triangles.

4 Measure the depth of a selection of pressed strip sets at various points along the length of the sets. Depending on the accuracy of your seam allowance, the sets should measure 4½ in/11.5 cm or thereabouts. Cut the background fabric into six strips that are the same depth as this measurement, cutting across the width of the fabric.

5 With right sides together, pin one background strip to one strip set, pinning along the long sides top and bottom. Stitch along both long sides, taking the usual seam allowance, to create a tube (diagram 2). Repeat with the other five strip sets and background strips. Press carefully with the seams closed.

diagram 2

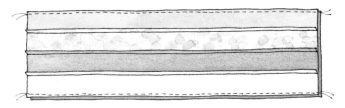

6 Place one of the tubes on the cutting mat. Note which strip is at the top, as it is important that this strip should be at the top when each tube is cut into triangles. Using a large rotary cutting ruler that has a 45° angle marked and working from the right-hand edge, line up the 45° angle along the top or bottom edge of the tube and cut with your rotary cutter (diagram 3).

diagram 3

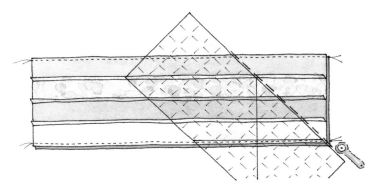

7 Turning the ruler, line the 45° angle along the top or bottom edge of the tube and cut in the opposite direction as shown in diagram 4. Continue cutting along the length of the tube to yield eight triangles.

diagram 4

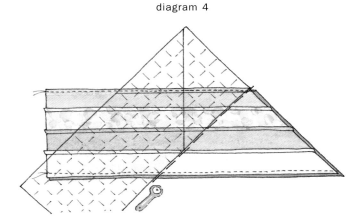

NOTE

If you can only cut six or seven triangles from each tube, sufficient yardage has been allowed for you to make an additional strip set from which to cut the extra triangles.

8 Repeat with the remaining tubes. Handle the triangles with care, as they have two bias edges.

9 Unpick the few threads at the top of the triangles (diagram 5) and open the blocks out. Press the seam allowance towards the background fabric. Trim the "ears", the small triangular ends that extend beyond the edges of the blocks.

diagram 5

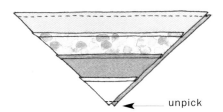

unpick

10 Following the quilt assembly diagram on page 20, lay out the blocks in eight rows of six blocks, alternating the two different blocks.

11 Stitch the blocks together in rows. If you press the seam allowances between the blocks in opposite directions for alternate rows, you will be able to butt them together when joining the rows, giving a neat fit with sharp points where the diagonals meet.

12 Stitch the rows together, then press the top lightly.

Adding the borders

1 Measure the pieced top through the centre from top to bottom, then trim two of the $4^{1}/_{2}$ in/11.5 cm deep borders to this length. Pin and stitch to the sides of the pieced top. Ease the borders to fit as necessary, but try not to stretch them too much. Press the seam allowances towards the borders.

2 Measure the pieced top through the centre from side to side, then trim the remaining two $4^{1}/_{2}$ in/11.5 cm deep borders to this length. Pin and stitch to the top and bottom of the pieced top. Press as before.

Finishing

1 Spread the backing right side down on a flat surface, then smooth out the wadding and the patchwork top, right side up, on top. Fasten together with safety pins or baste in a grid.

2 Mark the top with the desired quilting design. The quilt shown was marked in long diagonal lines with a plastic tool called a Hera marker and a long ruler; the marker makes an indentation in the layered quilt that shows up well on light-coloured fabric. The machine quilting lines run diagonally through the plain squares and also in the ditch between the longer strips; the quilting lines extend out into the borders. This is a simple yet pleasing way of securing the quilt layers.

3 Join the binding strips with diagonal seams to make a continuous length to fit all round the quilt and use to bind the edges with a double-fold binding, mitred at the corners.

Orchid
Wallhanging

DESIGNED
BY
Rita
Whitehorn

To give the raised effect of the orchid in its pot, I've cut the appliqué shapes in two layers of fabric. Alternatively, for a flatter look, the flowers, leaves, stem and pot can be cut in a single layer of fabric and appliquéd in the usual way.

Quilt assembly diagram

Finished size: 28 x 28 in/70 x 70 cm (excluding tabs)

Materials

All fabrics used in the quilt top are 45 in/115 cm wide, 100% cotton

For the squares and outer border: black and white print fabric, 24 in/60 cm

For the squares: white, 12 in/30 cm fabric

For the pot, inner border and binding: black, 26 in/65 cm

For the stem and leaves: green, 20 in/50 cm

For the flowers: fuchsia pink, 20 in/50 cm

Wadding: 31 x 31 in/79 x 79 cm square

Backing: 31 x 31 in/79 x 79 cm square

Fusible web: 10 in/25 cm

3 buttons

Silver thread

White and green quilting thread

Sewing thread: to match flowers, leaves, pot and for binding

Paper for templates

Cutting

1 From the black and white print fabric, cut eight 5½ in/14 cm squares; then cut four strips, 3 in/7.5 cm deep, across the width of the fabric for the outer border.

2 From the white fabric, cut eight 5½ in/14 cm squares.

3 From the black fabric, cut three strips, 1¾ in/4.5 cm deep, across the width of the fabric for the inner border; cut two rectangles, 6 x 5½ in/15.5 x 14 cm, for the orchid pot; cut four strips, 2 in/5 cm deep, across the width of the fabric for the binding.

4 Using the template paper, make templates for the stem, petals and leaves from the patterns on pages 30-31. Use the petal templates to cut 12 petal A shapes and 18 petal B shapes from the fuchsia pink fabric.

5 From the green fabric, cut a strip on the diagonal, 1½ in/4 cm wide and 12 in/30 cm long; using the paper templates, cut two leaf 1 shapes, two leaf 2 shapes, two leaf 3 shapes and two leaf 4 shapes.

27

Alternative colour schemes

1 This scheme conjures up an image of orchids amongst a collection of blue and white china.

2 Here, yellow orchids stand out against county cottage-style wallpaper.

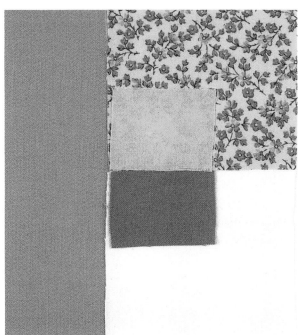

3 Cool colours make a sophisticated background to the yellow orchids in a green pot.

4 For a natural, toning room decoration, try this muted colour scheme.

Stitching

1 Following the quilt assembly diagram on page 26, lay out the squares in four rows of four squares, alternating the white with the black and white.

2 Stitch the squares together in rows and press the seams towards the black and white squares.

3 Stitch the rows together and press the seams downwards.

Adding the borders

1 For the inner border, cut one of the narrow black strips in half crosswise. Stitch one strip to each side of the pieced top and trim level. Press towards the border. Stitch the remaining two strips to the top and bottom. Trim level and press as before.

2 For the outer border, stitch one 3 in/7.5 cm black and white strip to each side of the pieced top and trim level. Press towards the inner border. Stitch the remaining two strips to the top and bottom. Trim and press as before.

Stitching the appliqué

1 To make the stem, place the paper template in position on the pieced top, following the quilt assembly diagram. Fold the green diagonal strip in half right side out and stitch a narrow seam just inside the raw edges, the length of the strip. Place the raw edges against the outer curve of the paper template, pin, then hand or machine in place. Remove the paper template, fold over the stem fabric, pin, then with matching thread and small stitches, appliqué in place (diagram 1).

diagram 1

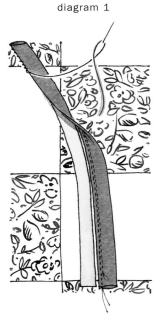

2 To make the pot, take one of the black rectangles and round off the two bottom corners on the longer side. Repeat for the second rectangle. Place the rectangles right sides together and stitch round all four sides, taking a narrow seam. Snip curves almost to the seam and make a cut in the back of the pot shape (diagram 2). Turn inside out through the cut, rolling the edges and pushing the corners out. Press. Cut a smaller pot shape from the fusible web and press onto the back of the pot shape, covering the cut. Remove the paper backing.

diagram 2

3 Position the pot to cover about $\frac{1}{2}$ in/1.5 cm of the bottom of the stem and press in place. Then, working from the back, catch stitch about $\frac{1}{4}$ in/0.75 cm in from the edges of the pot to hold it in position, taking care not to let the stitches show on the front of the work.

4 To make the leaves, place two leaf 2 shapes right sides together and stitch together round both sides, taking a narrow seam. Make a cut in the back and turn right side out. Apply with the fusible web in position at the bottom of the stem and overlapping the pot, then stitch from the back as before. Quilt a line along the centre leaves with green quilting thread. Repeat with the remaining leaves (diagram 3).

diagram 3

5 To make the flowers, place two petal B shapes right sides together and stitch all around with a narrow seam, starting on a long side, and proceed as for the leaves. Place two petal A shapes right sides together and stitch a narrow seam around the curved edge only. Snip the curves and turn inside out through the straight edge. Place the raw edges of the two petal A shapes together and stitch a small seam down the centre, Press open (diagram 4).

diagram 4

6 Pin the smaller petals in position on the stem, then place large petals over them. Adjust until satisfied with the arrangement. Stitch from the back as before, making sure that the petal A seam allowance doesn't show.

Sew the buttons in place with silver thread and tie; cut the thread to the required length (diagram 5).

diagram 5

Finishing

1 Spread the backing right side down on a flat surface, then smooth out the wadding and the pieced top, right side up, on top. Fasten together with safety pins or baste in a grid. Quilt around the pot, stem, leaves, flowers and white squares with white thread. Quilt in-the-ditch round the black border with black thread.

2 Trim off excess wadding and backing fabric in line with the quilt top. Press a $^1/_4$ in/0.75 cm turning along the long edge of the black binding strips. Place one strip on one side of the quilt top, right side down, and aligning the raw edges of the unfolded side with the raw edge of the quilt. Stitch, taking the usual seam allowance. Turn the binding over to the back of the quilt and hem stitch in place. Trim the binding level with the quilt edge. Repeat to bind the opposite side. Do the same to add the top and bottom binding, but turn a small amount of fabric in to neaten before stitching down.

3 To make the tabs, cut a strip from the remaining black fabric $5^1/_2$ in/14 cm wide across the width of the fabric. Fold in half, right sides together, and stitch with the usual seam allowance. Turn right side out and press with the seam in the centre. Cut crosswise into four $8^1/_2$ in/21.5 cm sections. Fold each small strip in half with the seam on the outside. Stitch across the short end, taking the usual seam allowance, press the seam open and turn the loop inside out. Position the tabs on the back of the quilt, leaving about 2 in/5 cm of loop showing above the binding. Hand stitch in place.

Templates

All 100% except where specified.

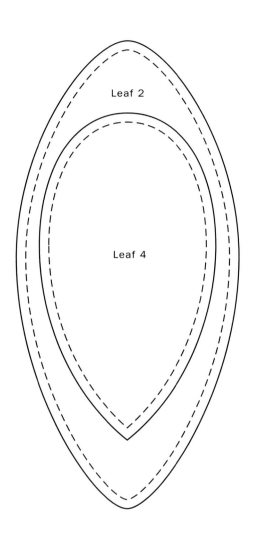

Leaf 2

Leaf 4

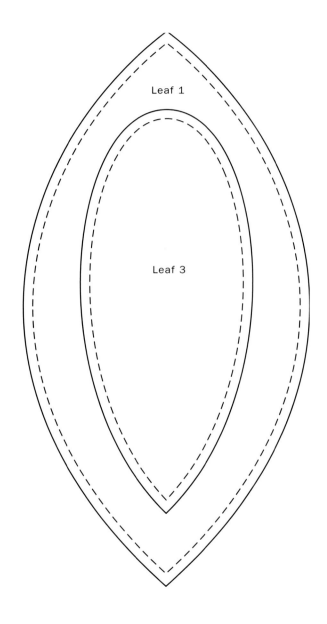

Leaf 1

Leaf 3

Stem

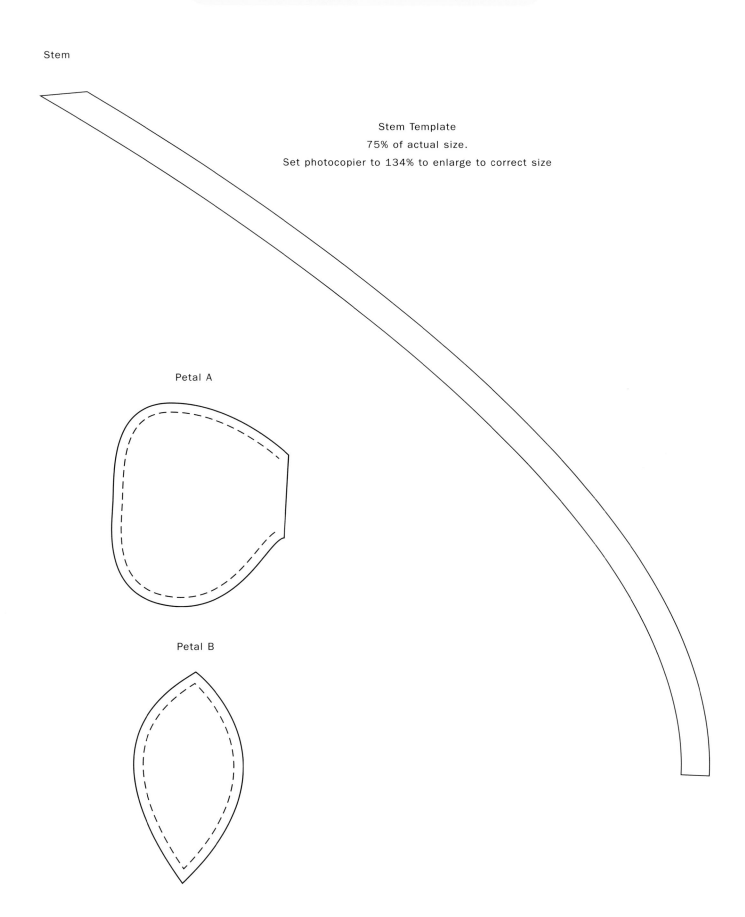

Stem Template

75% of actual size.

Set photocopier to 134% to enlarge to correct size

Petal A

Petal B

Rainbow Cot Quilt

DESIGNED
BY
Sarah Wellfair

When new bolts of fabric come into the shop, they are placed in stacks on the desk for pricing. They always look very appealing, and this particular set of batik fabrics gave me the idea for the bars of colour in this little cot quilt. I've used the sashing to break up the coloured bars and have added four borders to enhance the rainbow effect.

Quilt assembly diagram

Finished size: 40 x 44 in/101 x 104 cm

Materials

All fabrics used in the quilt top are 45 in/115 cm wide, 100% cotton

For the strips: seven long quarters of bright colours (each approximately 10 x 45 in/25 x 115 cm)

Sashing: ivory on ivory print, 20 in/50 cm
Wadding: lightweight, 44 x 48 in/111 x 114 cm
Backing: 44 x 48 in/111 x 114 cm
Thread to match for sewing and quilting

Alternative colour schemes

1 A mix of soft batiks with a black border.

2 Bright yellows, pinks and greens are vibrant.

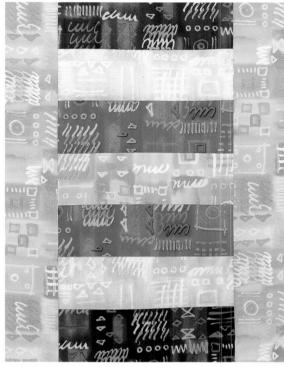

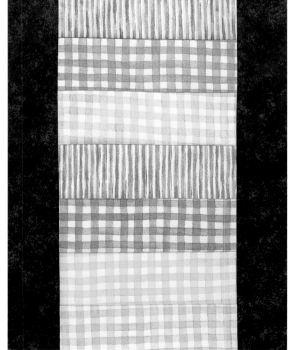

3 Cottage-garden, floral prints with a cream star contrast create a softer look.

4 Plaids, checks and stripes with a blue border look very fresh.

Cutting

1 From each of the seven long quarters, cut one strip, $2^{1}/_{2}$ in/6 cm deep, across the width of the fabric for the centre coloured blocks. Select four of the long quarters for the borders and cut four strips, $1^{1}/_{2}$ in/4 cm deep, across the width from each. From two of the remaining long quarters, cut two strips, $2^{1}/_{4}$ in/5.5 cm deep, across the width from each for the binding.

2 From the sashing fabric, cut six strips, 3 in/7.5 cm deep, across the width of the fabric.

Stitching

1 Arrange the strips cut from the long quarters in the order in which you wish to stitch them together.

2 Take the first two strips, place right sides together and stitch down one long edge, taking a $^{1}/_{4}$ in/0.75 cm seam. Press the seams towards the first strip.

3 Continue adding strips in the same way, always pressing the seams in the same direction. You should now have seven coloured strips sewn together.

4 Place this strip unit on a cutting board and cut off the selvage from one side. Now, using ruler and cutter, cross-cut six 7 in/18 cm sections (diagram 1).

diagram 1

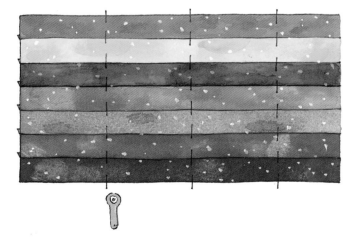

5 Take two of these strips and place right sides together so that the top of the first strip lies over the bottom of the second. Stitch together along one short edge (diagram 2). Do the same to the other strips. You should have three multi-coloured strips.

diagram 2

6 Measure each block down the length and take an average measurement of length.

7 Trim four of the 3 in/7.5 cm wide sashing strips to this measurement.

8 Stitch one sashing strip to each long side of one multi-coloured strip. Turn the next multi-coloured strip upside down, then add to the right-hand sashing strip, following diagram 3. Press the seams towards the sashing. Continue to add sashing strips and the final multi-coloured strip.

diagram 3

9 Measure the pieced top through the centre from side to side, then trim the remaining two sashing strips to this measurement. Stitch to the top and bottom of the pieced top.

Adding the borders

1 Take four $1^{1}/_{2}$ in/4 cm wide border strips of one colour. Measure the pieced top through the centre from top to bottom, then trim two of the border strips to this measurement. Stitch to the sides of the pieced top (diagram 4).

diagram 4

2 Measure the pieced top through the centre from side to side, then trim the remaining two sashing strips of the same colour to this measurement. Stitch to the top and bottom of the pieced top.

3 Take the second set of four border strips and stitch to the pieced top in the same way, always measuring through the centre, as this will keep your quilt square and flat. Repeat with the third and fourth sets of border strips.

Finishing

1 Spread the backing right side down on a flat surface, then smooth out the wadding and the pieced top, right side up, on top. Fasten together with safety pins or baste in a grid.

2 Quilt in-the-ditch round the blocks and borders.

3 Take two binding strips of the same colour, fold in half down the length and press.

4 Measure the quilt through the centre from top to bottom, then trim each of the strips to this length. Stitch to the sides of the pieced top, right sides together and matching the raw edges. Flip the binding to the reverse of the pieced top and slip stitch in place along the stitching line.

5 Measure the pieced top through the centre from side to side, add $1^{1}/_{2}$ in/4 cm to this measurement, then trim each of the remaining two binding strips to this length. Fold in half and press as before. Stitch to the top and bottom of the quilt, leaving $^{3}/_{4}$ in/2 cm over at either end. Turn in the ends of binding, flip to the back and slip stitch in place as before.

Spider's Web Cot Quilt

DESIGNED
BY
Mary
O'Riordan

This string-pieced quilt puts narrow scraps of fabric to good use, so it has great design potential for quilters with an organized stash of scrap fabrics. The strips are stitched onto a foundation fabric to produce bigger, more manageable units.

Quilt assembly diagram

Finished size: 32 x 42 in/82 x 108 cm

Materials

All fabrics used in the quilt top are 45 in/115 cm wide, 100% cotton

For the background: white, 1⅓ yds/1.2 m

For the spider's webs: printed fabrics in a selection of bright colours to total 1⅔ yds/1.5 m (I've used 11 different patterns)

Binding: striped fabric, 24 in/30 cm

Backing: 38 x 48 in/96 x 122 cm

Wadding: 38 x 48 in/96 x 122 cm

Template plastic

Alternative colour schemes

1 Use two contrasting fabrics for the background foundation triangles to create a spider's web pinwheel.

2 Using only two fabrics and strips in two widths produces an interesting effect with lots of movement in the stripes.

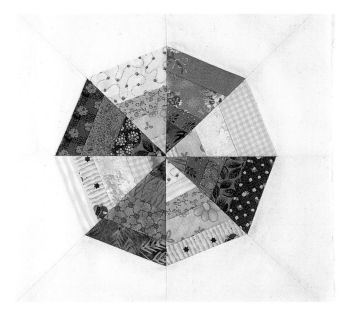

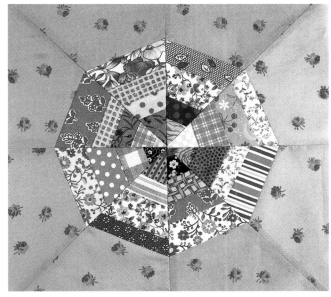

3 A whole new look is achieved by separating the segments of the octagon by subtle colour contrasts. This version is Spider's Windmill.

4 Choose a vintage-style floral fabric with coordinating prints, checks, spots and stripes for a fresh look.

Cutting

1 From white background fabric, cut 24 squares measuring 8½ in/22 cm. Cut these in half on the diagonal to make 48 foundation triangles.

2 Cut the printed fabric into strips across the width of the fabric, varying the depth from 1 to 2 in/2.5 to 5 cm.

3 Cut the binding fabric into four strips, 2½ in/6.5 cm deep, across the width of the fabric.

4 Trace the template below onto the template plastic and cut out.

Stitching the blocks

1 Place the template on one of the foundation triangles, aligning the right angles, and mark along the edge of the template with a pencil.

Template

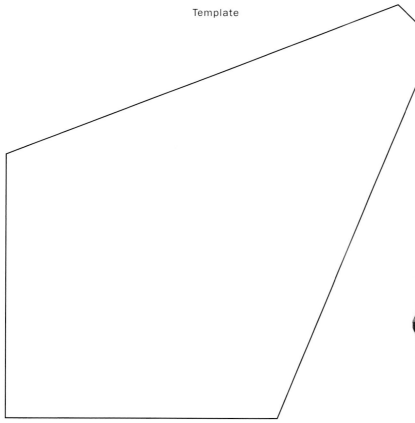

2 From one of the strips of printed fabric, cut a piece about 5 in/14 cm long and line it up against the marked line on the foundation triangle, right sides together. Stitch, taking a ¼ in/0.75 cm seam allowance (diagram 1).

diagram 1

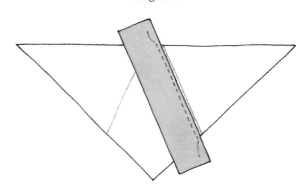

NOTE

It is important to stitch an accurate ¼ in/0.75 cm seam allowance when you attach the first strip to the foundation triangle, so that the outside edges of the spider's web match up when joined later.

3 Finger press the strip towards the point. Cut the next strip from a different fabric long enough to extend slightly beyond the sides of the foundation triangle. Align with the edge of the first strip, right sides together, and stitch in place. Flip open and finger press towards the point. Continue the process until the end of the foundation triangle is covered completely (diagram 2).

diagram 2

4 Work on the other side of the foundation triangle in the same way, lining up the first strip against the marked line and stitching with an accurate $^1/_4$ in/0.75 cm seam (diagram 3).

diagram 3

5 Press the triangle when both sides are covered. Lay the piece right side down on a cutting board and trim the strips even with the sides of the foundation triangle. Repeat to make a total of 48 triangle units.

6 Stitch four triangle units together to form a block, being careful to match up the points where the strips meet to create the edge of the spider's web (diagram 4).

diagram 4

7 Press seams open to distribute the bulk. Repeat to make a total of 12 blocks.

8 Following the quilt assembly diagram on page 40, stitch three blocks together to form a row, then stitch the rows together to complete the pieced top.

Finishing

1 Spread the backing right side down on a flat surface, then smooth out the wadding and the patchwork top, right side up, on top. Fasten together with safety pins or baste in a grid.

2 Quilt $^1/_4$ in/0.75 cm from the seam line on the background fabric and inside the segments of the spider's web. Trim the excess wadding and backing level with the pieced top.

3 Join the binding strips with diagonal seams to make a continuous length to fit all round the quilt and use to bind the edges with a double-fold binding, mitred at the corners.

Miniature Log Cabin Wallhanging

DESIGNED
BY
Katharine
Guerrier

The trend towards a more asymmetrical approach to quilts is exploited in this wallhanging. The strips are cut in an improvisational way, creating the effect of movement with their uneven widths. Strips are stitched, then trimmed as the block is built, so accuracy is not required when stitching the seams, and piecing is fairly easy.

Quilt assembly diagram

Finished size: $21^{1}/_{2}$ x $21^{1}/_{2}$ in/55 x 55 cm

Materials

All fabrics used in the quilt top are 45 in/115 cm wide, 100% cotton

Yellow: 4 in/10 cm

Black: 20 in/50 cm

Green: 20 in/50 cm (including the binding)

Pink and turquoise: 9 in/25 cm

Wadding: 2 oz or low loft, 24 x 24 in/61 x 61 cm

Backing: cotton, 24 x 24 in/61 x 61 cm

Machine quilting thread

Cutting

1 From the yellow fabric and using scissors, cut 36 squares for the block centres, measuring between 1 and $1^{1}/_{4}$ in/2.5 and 3 cm square – don't worry if they are not true squares. Aim for corners that are not necessarily 90 ° angles. (The strips for the "logs" are cut as you need them.)

2 From the green fabric, cut four strips, $2^{1}/_{4}$ x 22 in/5.75 x 55 cm, for the binding.

Alternative colour schemes

1 In this variation, the block centres are made with the more frequently used traditional, red fabric.

2 Purple and green are analogous on the colour wheel and will always work well together.

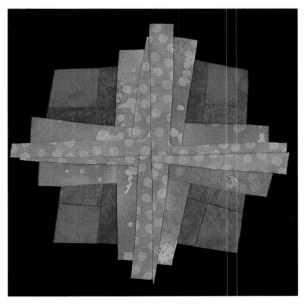

3 Pastel florals teamed with a mid blue make a block with less contrast between the light and dark sides.

4 Fun prints in fuchsia pink and electric blue for a stunning effect.

Stitching

1 To make the blocks, cut two strips of pink, 1¼ in/3 cm deep, across the width of the fabric.

2 Place the yellow centre squares right sides down along the right side of one of the pink strips, with a space of about ¼ in/0.75 cm between them and aligning raw edges. Stitch the centre squares to the strip using a narrow seam allowance of no more than ⅛ in/3 mm. Use a smaller stitch than for regular sewing (diagram 1).

diagram 1

3 Cut the strip into sections between the centre squares and press the seams towards the centre square. Trim the short edge of the pink level with the edge of the centre squares on the right-hand side.

4 Turn the centre squares by a quarter turn and place these units right sides down on the remaining pink strip. Stitch as in step 1 (diagram 2). Cut the strip into sections again, press and trim.

diagram 2

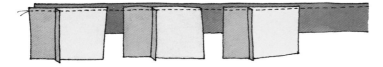

5 Now repeat steps 2 to 4, turning the unit by a quarter turn each time and using strips of black fabric cut 1¼ in/2.5 cm wide to complete the first round.

6 Trim the blocks, cutting the outer edges at skewed angles to the seams and leaving the width of the strips somewhere between ½ and ¾ in/1.25 and 2 cm. It does not matter at this stage if the blocks are all slightly different sizes (diagram 3).

diagram 3

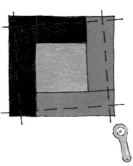

7 Add the second round in the same way, using the green fabric instead of the pink and the black. Trim as before (diagram 4).

diagram 4

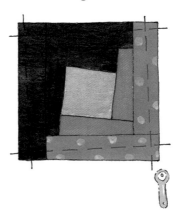

8 Now add the third round, using the turquoise and the black. Press all the blocks and trim them down to exact 4 in/10 cm squares (diagram 5).

diagram 5

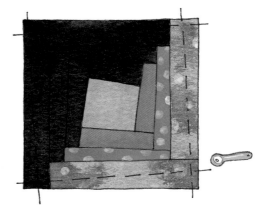

9 Repeat to make a total of 36 blocks.

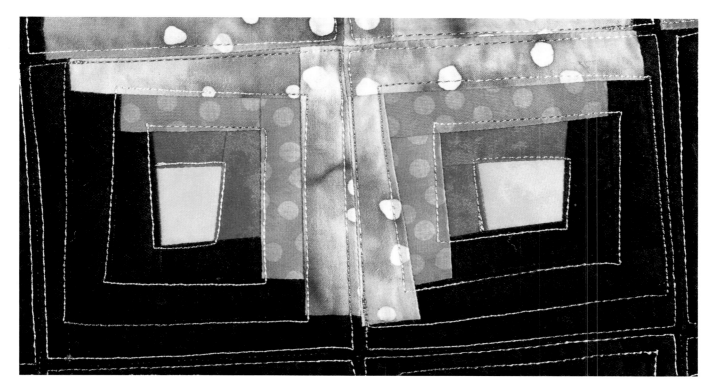

10 Stitch the blocks together in groups of four, taking a $^1/_4$ in/0.75 cm seam allowance. Press the seams open (diagram 6).

diagram 6

11 Following the quilt assembly diagram on page 46, stitch the sets of four blocks together to make the pieced top.

Finishing

1 Spread the backing right side down on a flat surface, then smooth out the wadding and the patchwork top, right side up, on top. Fasten together with safety pins or baste in a grid.

2 Quilt by machine, stitching close to the seams around the centre squares and between the strips in a spiral on each block. Trim the wadding and backing close to the outer edges.

3 Fold the binding strips in half lengthwise, right sides together, and press. Place one strip along one side of the quilt, aligning raw edges, trim to fit and stitch taking the usual seam allowance. Fold to the back of the quilt and hem stitch in place along the stitching line. Repeat on the opposite side.

4 For the remaining two sides, stitch the strips to the quilt in the same way but, before folding to the back, trim the strips so that they are $^1/_4$ in/0.75 cm longer than the quilt at each end. Fold in the short overlap, then fold the binding to the back and hem stitch in place.

Lilac and Lavender Throw

DESIGNED
BY
Alison Wood

Using the Mitred Square block gives a crisp geometric look to this large throw or lap quilt. Speedy and accurate rotary cutting and machine piecing mean that the blocks fit together surprisingly easily. The key to success with this design is to have a good contrast between the light and dark fabrics with a linking or accent fabric in between.

Quilt assembly diagram

Finished size: 68 x 68 in/173 x 173 cm

Avoid choosing strongly directional or striped fabrics for this quilt and only use plaids if you don't mind a relaxed, "off-grain" look.

NOTE

The white calico used in the quilt top is 60 in/154 cm wide. Because you will be working with strips cut across the width of the fabric and pieced along the length of the strips, the same amount is needed as of the 45 in/115 cm fabrics, leaving offcuts to use in another project.

Materials

For the blocks: 2 yds/2 m of 45 in/115 cm (minimum width) of each of three fabrics in light, medium and dark shades

Binding: an extra 20 in/50 cm of the darkest fabric

Backing: 4 yds/3.75 m of 45 in/115 cm wide fabric

Wadding: Approximately 72 x 92 in/183 x 234 cm (twin or single size). Cotton or 80:20 cotton/polyester mix is more suitable for machine quilting. For hand quilting, use either cotton/cotton blend or 2 oz polyester

Alternative colour schemes

1 The design could be minimal in black and white with a red accent.

2 A lively design in zingy brights.

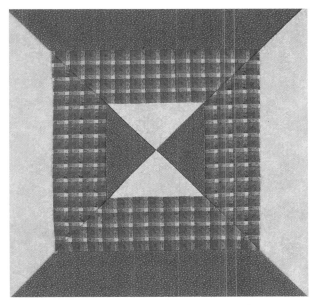

3 Blue and white is crisp but restful.

4 Soft floral fabrics give a less sharply defined country look.

Cutting

1 From each of the three main fabrics, cut 32 strips, 2 in/5 cm deep, across the width of the fabric.

2 Cut the binding fabric into seven strips, $2\frac{1}{2}$ in/6 cm deep, across the width of the fabric.

Stitching

1 Stitch one dark strip to one medium strip, right sides together, along the length of the strips, taking an accurate $\frac{1}{4}$ in/0.75 cm seam allowance. Take care not to stretch the strips as you stitch them, as this can lead to bowing and distortion.

2 Repeat with all the other dark and medium strips: remember to be consistent about which fabric you have on top as you stitch the strips together so that you always have the dark fabric attached to the same side of the medium fabric. Chain piecing the strips will save time and thread.

3 Press the seam joining the pairs of strips flat first; this "sets" the seam, causing the thread to sink into the fabric a little, which helps to give a flatter, crisper finish. Then, with the dark fabric on top, use the side of the iron to gently flip over and press the dark fabric away from the medium fabric, pressing on the right side to ensure there are no little pleats beside the seam. Try to press, not to iron the fabric, as you do not want to curve the stitched strip unit.

4 Now, stitch one light strip to the medium fabric side of the unit, again putting right sides together and keeping to a $\frac{1}{4}$ in/0.75 cm seam allowance. Repeat with all the remaining light strips. Press towards the medium fabric.

5 If you have pre-washed your fabrics or they are only lightly dressed, you may wish at this stage to lightly mist the strip sets with spray starch from the right side and press carefully. This will help to stabilize the bias edges, which will be exposed by the next stage.

6 Take two strip sets and place one on the cutting mat right side up and with the light strip at the top. Place the second unit on top, right sides together and upside down, so that the dark strip lies on top of the light strip

and vice versa (diagram 1). If you have stitched accurately and pressed carefully, you should be able to feel the seam allowances interlock or butt together.

diagram 1

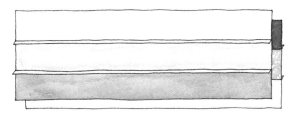

7 Using a large rotary cutting ruler and working from the right-hand end of the pair of strip sets, line up the 45° angle along the top or bottom edge and cut (diagram 2).

diagram 2

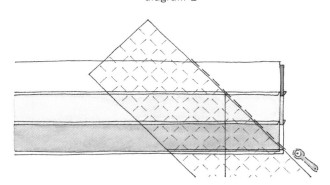

8 Turning the ruler and lining the 45° line up with the top or bottom edge of the pair of strip sets, cut in the opposite direction as shown in diagram 3 to give a pair of triangle units. Make sure that the two cut lines intersect at the tip of the triangle. Continue cutting along

NOTE

Each of the 16 pairs of strip sets may yield seven pairs of triangle units, which will be stitched together into 56 blocks. These will make a slightly smaller quilt, with 7 rows of 8 blocks. However, there is enough spare fabric in the amounts specified to make two extra pairs of strip sets to yield eight more blocks.

the length of the strip sets to yield seven (or possibly eight) pairs of triangle units.

diagram 3

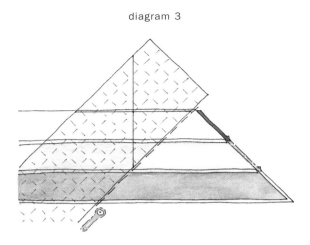

9 Keeping the pairs together, stitch carefully along one of the diagonal edges of each pair (diagram 4): remember that each triangle has two bias edges and handle them with care.

diagram 4

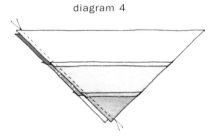

10 Repeat the directions for cutting all the remaining strip sets into triangles and then stitch all the pairs of triangle units together. You need a total of 128 triangle units.

11 Press all the pairs of triangle units carefully; set the seams and then press the seam allowance to one side, working from the right side. If you press all units in the same direction, it will make it easier when you come to join the blocks.

12 Take two joined pairs of triangle units and place right sides together, butting up the centre seams, which should fit together neatly. Visually, the most important place for accuracy is the centre seam. Pin and stitch the long diagonal bias edge. Join all the remaining units (diagram 5).

diagram 5

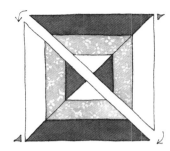

13 Press to set the seams and then press to one side from the right side. Trim off the small triangular "ears" that extend beyond the edges of the block.

14 Stitch the blocks together in pairs, then into fours and finally rows of eight blocks, butting the seam allowances wherever possible. If you press the seam allowances between the blocks in opposite directions for alternate rows, you will be able to butt them together when joining the rows, giving a neat fit with sharp points where the diagonals meet.

15 Stitch the rows together, then press the top lightly.

Finishing

1 Measure the completed quilt top and, if necessary, cut and piece the backing to fit with at least 2 in/5 cm all round. If you are joining the backing, don't forget to cut off the selvages, as these are very tightly woven and can cause distortion in the quilt. Press the seam open.

2 Spread the backing right side down on a flat surface, then smooth out the wadding and the patchwork top, right side up, on top. Fasten together with safety pins or baste in a grid.

3 Mark the top with the desired quilting design. I machine quilted in-the-ditch along the seams joining the blocks together, then quilted in long diagonal lines in-the-ditch beside the diagonal seams.

4 Join the binding strips with diagonal seams to make a continuous length to fit all round the quilt and use to bind the edges with a double-fold binding, mitred at the corners.

Jacob's Ladder Quilt

DESIGNED BY Mary O'Riordan

Jacob's Ladder is a traditional quilt block that offers easy construction and infinite design possibilities. This version emphasizes the diagonal nature of the block. The fabrics, set against the white background, suggest over-sized candy wrappers.

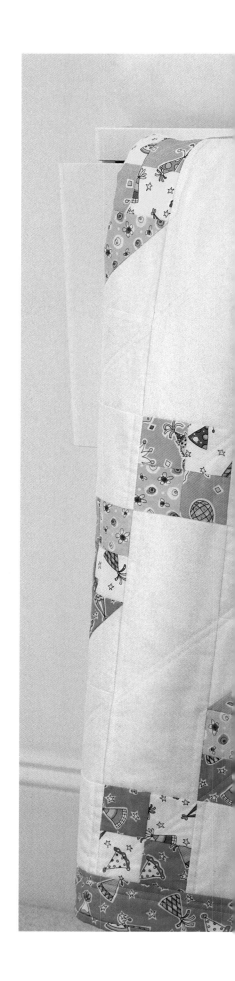

Quilt assembly diagram

Finished size: 56½ x 72½ in/140 x 180 cm

Materials

All fabrics used in the quilt top are 45 in/115 cm wide, 100% cotton

For the background and sashing: white on white fabric, 2⅓ yds/2 m

For the blocks and sashing posts: four bright prints in blue, yellow, green and pink, 2 yds /1.9 m

For the border and binding: an extra 1 yd/1 m of the blue print

Wadding: 62 x 78 in/155 x 195 cm

Backing: 62 x 78 in/155 x 195 cm

Alternative colour schemes

1 To create a light and airy mood, choose softly contrasting pastels.

2 Red and white is a classic combination. Highlighting different areas of the block gives a variety of interesting results.

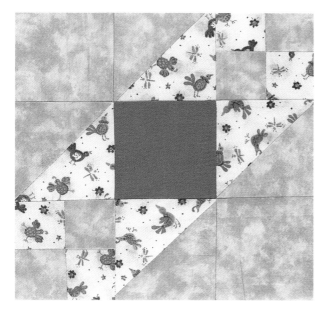

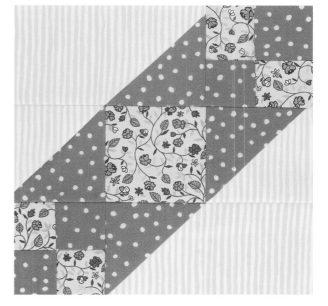

3 Find an exciting fabric for the background and use it also for the centre square to make a window in the diagonal.

4 Spots, stripes and floral prints combine well for most colourways to give a lively feel.

Cutting

1 From the white fabric, cut 12 strips, $4^{1}/_{2}$ in/11.5 cm deep, across the width of the fabric. Cross-cut to produce 31 rectangles, $4^{1}/_{2}$ x $12^{1}/_{2}$ in/11.5 x 31.5 cm, and 24 squares measuring $4^{1}/_{2}$ in/11.5 cm. Cut three strips, $4^{7}/_{8}$ in/12.5 cm deep, across the width of the fabric. Cross-cut to produce 24 squares measuring $4^{7}/_{8}$ in/12.5 cm.

2 From the print fabrics, cut 12 strips, $2^{1}/_{2}$ in/6.5 cm deep, across the width of fabric for the four-patch units. Cut 4 strips, $4^{7}/_{8}$ in /12.5 cm deep, across the width of the fabric and cross-cut to produce 24 squares, $4^{7}/_{8}$ in/ 12.5 cm. Trim the remaining strips to $4^{1}/_{2}$ in/11.5 cm deep and cross-cut to produce 12 squares, $4^{1}/_{2}$ in/11.5 cm.

3 From the border fabric, cut six strips, $2^{1}/_{2}$ in/6.5 cm deep, across the width of the fabric.

4 From the binding fabric, cut eight strips, $2^{1}/_{2}$ in/6.5 cm deep, across the width of the fabric.

Stitching

1 Stitch the $2^{1}/_{2}$ in/6.5 cm wide print strips together in pairs of different colours, right sides together, down one long edge, taking an accurate $^{1}/_{4}$ in/0.75 cm seam allowance. Press flat on the stitching line to relax the stitching, then press the seam towards the darker fabric.

2 Cross-cut the pieced strips at $2^{1}/_{2}$ in/6.5 cm intervals to produce 88 two-patch units (diagram 1).

diagram 1

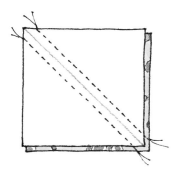

3 Chain stitch random pairs together to produce 44 four-patch units for the blocks and the sashing posts (diagram 2). Press.

diagram 2

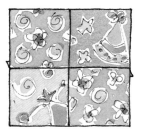

4 On the white $4^{7}/_{8}$ in/12.5 cm squares mark the diagonal in pencil on the wrong side of the fabric. Place a white $4^{7}/_{8}$ in/12.5 cm square on a print $4^{7}/_{8}$ in/12.5 cm square, right sides together, and stitch $^{1}/_{4}$ in/0.75 cm away on either side of the marked line (diagram 3).

diagram 3

NOTE

Check that the stitching lines are an accurate $^{1}/_{2}$ in/1.5 cm apart before cutting between them.

5 Cut along the marked line. Press towards the print fabric and trim the corners. The resulting half-triangle squares should measure $4^{1}/_{2}$ in/11.5 cm. Repeat to make 48 half-triangle squares.

6 Set out the four-patch units, half-triangle squares and plain squares in the block pattern (diagram 4). Stitch the blocks together first in rows, then stitch the rows together to form the block.

diagram 4

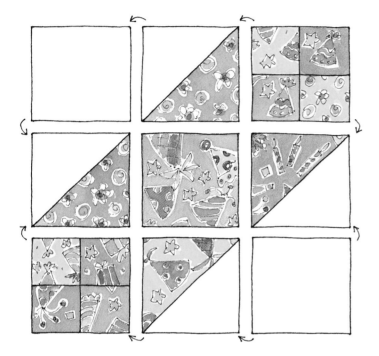

7 Following the quilt assembly diagram on page 58, stitch four rows of three blocks together with a white 4$^{1}/_{2}$ x 12$^{1}/_{2}$ in/11.5 x 31.5 cm sashing strip at the beginning and end, and between each block.

8 Stitch five rows of sashing strips and sashing posts together, three strips and four posts in each row, beginning and ending with a post.

9 Join the rows of blocks and sashing to complete the pieced top.

10 Join the six border strips into one long length. Measure the pieced top through the centre from top to bottom, then cut two border strips to this measurement. Stitch to the sides of the quilt. Press seams towards the borders.

11 Measure the pieced top through the centre from side to side, then cut two more border strips to this measurement. Stitch to the top and bottom. Press seams towards the borders.

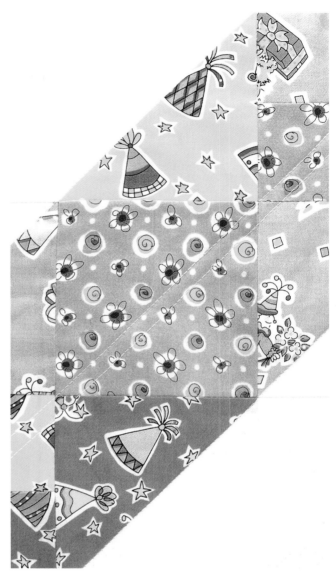

Finishing

1 Spread the backing right side down on a flat surface, then smooth out the wadding and the patchwork top, right side up, on top. Fasten together with safety pins or baste in a grid.

2 Quilt in-the-ditch vertically and horizontally along the sashing. Quilt the blocks $^{1}/_{4}$ in/0.75 cm away from the diagonal seams. Trim the excess wadding and backing level with the pieced top.

3 Join the binding strips with diagonal seams to make a continuous length to fit all round the quilt and use to bind the edges with a double-fold binding, mitred at the corners.

Modern Strippy Throw

DESIGNED
BY
Katharine
Guerrier

The "Strippy" is brought up-to-date with a bold design in which each of the strips has a detail of triangles arranged as rectangles. Pastel blue links the two fabrics used for the triangle detail, one of which is a larger scale print to add visual texture. Further interest is provided with narrow strips in high contrasting colours to add sparkle and warmth. It was quilted on a long-arm quilting machine by Jan Chandler.

Quilt assembly diagram

Finished size: 48 x 59 in/122 x 150 cm

Materials

All fabrics used in the quilt top are 45 in/115 cm wide, 100% cotton

For the trianges: yellow and pale blue prints, 20 in/50 cm of each

For the vertical strips: blue and turquoise space-dyed fabric, 30 in/75 cm of each

For the horizontal stripes: orange, pink and navy prints, 10 in/25 cm of each

Wadding: 2 oz or low loft, 56 x 67 in/143 x 171 cm

Backing: cotton, a piece 56 x 67 in/143 x 171 cm

Machine quilting thread

Binding: dark pink print, 20 in/50 cm

Alternative colour schemes

1 Use a variety of small dot prints in bright, contrasting shades and values for a colourful lap quilt.

2 Japanese prints add style and elegance to any project.

3 Realistic animal prints will contribute to an African-themed room.

4 If you have experimented with hand-dyeing fabrics, this is a good showcase for the results.

Cutting

1 From the yellow and pale blue printed fabrics, cut three rectangles, each 9¼ x 13¼ in/23.5 x 33.75 cm, for the triangles.

NOTE

Do not cut the blue and turquoise strips until the triangle blocks are made, to adjust the width if necessary.

2 From each of the orange, pink and navy fabrics, cut two strips, 2½ in/6.5 cm deep, across the width of the fabric.

3 From the binding fabric, cut five strips, 3 in/7.5 cm deep, across the width.

Stitching

1 Place one pale blue and one yellow rectangle right sides uppermost, then cross-cut across both diagonals (diagram 1).

2 Arrange the resulting triangles into two rectangles, with alternate prints for the triangles, then stitch into blocks as illustrated (diagram 2).

diagram 1

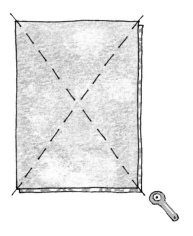

diagram 2

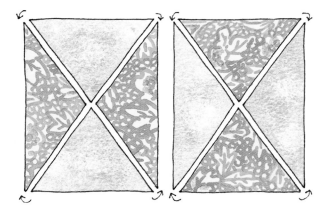

3 Repeat with the other two pairs to make six rectangles altogether.

4 Stitch the orange, navy and pink strips together along the long sides, with the navy strip in the middle and taking a $^1/_4$ in/0.75 cm seam allowance. Press the seams towards the navy. Measure the width of the triangle blocks, then cross-cut the strip set into six units of the same measurement (diagram 3).

diagram 3

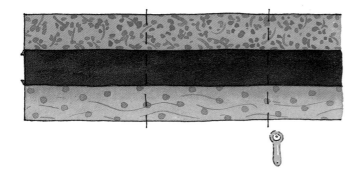

5 Use the same measurement to cut three strips to this depth from each of the turquoise and blue fabrics across the width of the fabric.

6 Following the quilt assembly diagram on page 64, cut the blue and turquoise strips into two or three lengths each and insert the triangle blocks and strip units at random intervals, alternating the blue and turquoise sections. Each long strip should measure roughly 61 in/155 cm.

7 Stitch the sections together into strips, then stitch the strips together. Trim the top and bottom edges level.

Finishing

1 If you plan to do your own quilting, spread the backing right side down on a flat surface, then smooth the wadding and the quilt top, right sides up on top. Fasten together with safety pins or baste in a grid.

2 Using the free motion quilting method, quilt over the whole surface in machine quilting thread.

3 Join the binding strips to make two lengths of 50 in/127.25 cm and two lengths of 61 in/155.25 cm. Use to bind the edges with a double-fold binding with squared corners.

Hexagon Flowers

DESIGNED BY Rita Whitehorn

I based the colour scheme for this bright throw on the striped fabric by picking out plain coloured fabrics to coordinate with the stripes. The little hexagon flowers are hand-stitched together in the traditional "Grandmother's Flower Garden" design before being appliquéed to the quilt.

Quilt assembly diagram

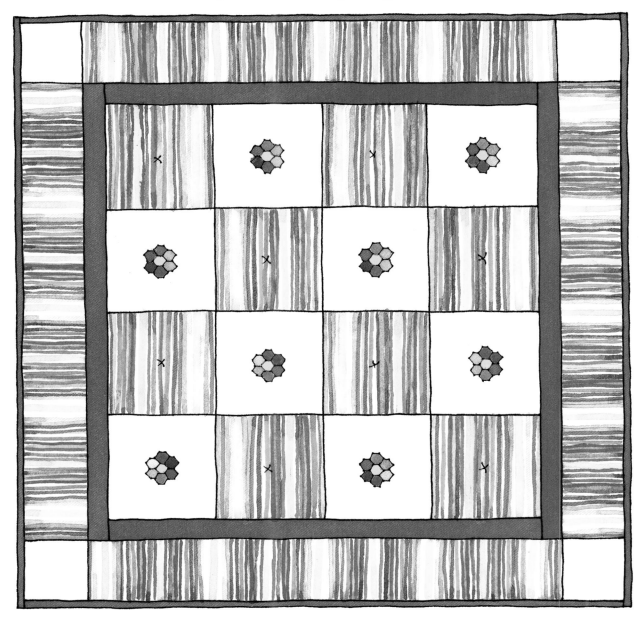

Finished size: 56½ x 56½ in/142 x 142 cm

Materials

All fabrics used in the quilt top are 45 in/115 cm wide, 100% cotton

Multi-coloured stripe: 1⅔ yds/1.25 m

Hexagons: one 12 x 4 in/36 x 10 cm rectangle of each of the six plain colours to coordinate with the multi-coloured stripe

Inner border, binding and hexagons: 1 yd/90 cm of a seventh plain colour to coordinate with the multi-coloured stripe

White fabric: 30 in/75 cm

Template plastic

Paper for templates

Backing: patterned pink, 3⅓ yds/3.10 m or one piece, 60 in/152 cm square

Pale grey sewing cotton

Wadding: lightweight, 60 x 60 in/152 x 152 cm

White pearl cotton embroidery thread

Alternative colour schemes

1 The strong, multi-coloured fabric will produce a bold design.

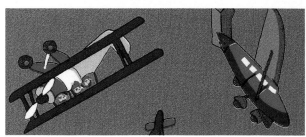

2 The soft pastels of the sweet peas are echoed in the hexagon flowers.

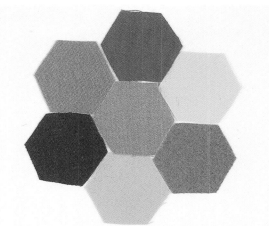

3 The novelty fabric and the coordinating plain colours make a bright design for a boy's room.

4 Keeping all the fabrics within one colour range produces a warm and comforting design.

Cutting

1 Using the templates below, cut one large hexagon (which includes the seam allowance) from template plastic and one smaller one (which is the finished size of the hexagon). Using the smaller template, cut 56 hexagons from the paper.

2 From the multi-coloured stripe, cut four strips, $6\frac{1}{2}$ in/16.5 cm deep, across the width of fabric for the outer border, taking care that the stripes are straight. Trim off the selvages. Cut eight $10\frac{1}{2}$ in/26.5 cm squares for the quilt centre.

3 From the border and binding fabric, cut four strips, $2\frac{1}{2}$ in/6.5 cm deep, across the width of the fabric for the inner border. Trim off the selvages. The remaining fabric is used for the hexagon flowers and the binding.

4 From each of the seven plain, coloured fabrics (i.e. including the border and binding fabric) and using the larger plastic template, cut eight hexagons.

5 From the white fabric, cut eight $10\frac{1}{2}$ in/26.5 cm squares for the quilt centre; cut four $6\frac{1}{2}$ in/16.5 cm squares for the outer border corners.

6 From the backing fabric, cut two rectangles, $30\frac{1}{2}$ x 60 in/77 x 152 cm.

Stitching

1 Pin a hexagon paper shape to the wrong side of one of the fabric hexagons, fold over the seam allowance on one edge and tack or baste. Fold over the adjacent edge and do the same. Repeat with all six sides (diagram 1).

diagram 1

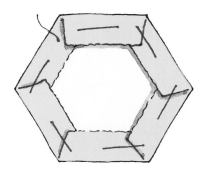

2 Do the same with the remaining 55 hexagon paper shapes, so that you have eight sets of seven hexagons of different colours.

3 Take one set of seven hexagons and arrange them in a pleasing colour sequence into a flower shape.

4 Using the pale grey thread, place the centre hexagon shape right sides together with one of the petal hexagons and oversew along one edge, taking up just a tiny amount of seam allowance (diagram 2).

diagram 2

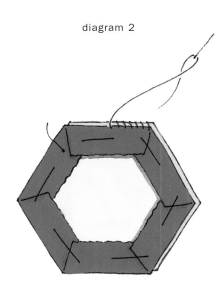

Templates

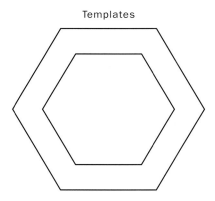

5 Without breaking the thread, take the next adjacent petal hexagon, place right sides together with the centre hexagon, oversew along the edge adjacent to the previous one and fasten off. Then, realign this second petal hexagon, so that it is right sides together with the first, and oversew the adjoining edges (diagram 3).

diagram 3

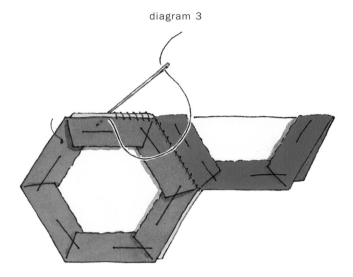

6 Continue in this way, adding petal hexagons until all seven have been stitched to each other and the central hexagon. The final hexagon will also need to be stitched to the first. Press on the wrong side, remove tacking or basting stitches and take out the papers. Repeat to make a total of eight hexagon flowers.

7 Fold the white squares in half, then half again; do not press, but just pinch the centre points. Place a pin in the centre of one of the hexagon flowers and line this up with the centre of white square, then pin all around the shape. Using pale grey thread, appliqué the flower in position using a tiny hem stitch.

8 Following the quilt assembly diagram on page 70, lay out the appliquéed squares, alternating them with the striped squares in four rows of four squares. Pin and stitch the squares together, first in rows, then pin and stitch the rows together.

Adding the borders

1 To add the inner border, measure the pieced top through the centre from side to side, then trim two of the $2\frac{1}{2}$ in/6 cm strips to this measurement. Stitch to the top and bottom. Measure the pieced top through the centre from top to bottom, then trim the remaining two strips to this measurement. Pin and stitch to the sides.

2 To add the outer border, measure the pieced top through the centre from side to side, then trim the four $6\frac{1}{2}$ in/16.5 cm strips to this measurement. Pin and stitch one strip to the top and one to the bottom of the quilt. Stitch one of the white $6\frac{1}{2}$ in/16.5 cm squares to either end of the remaining two border strips, then stitch to the sides of the pieced top, matching seams carefully.

Finishing

1 Stitch the two rectangles for the backing fabric together down one long side, taking the usual seam allowance.

2 Spread the backing right side down on a flat surface, then smooth out the wadding and the patchwork top, right side up, on top. Fasten together with safety pins or baste in a grid.

3 Quilt by hand or machine around the hexagon flowers. Quilt in-the-ditch on either side of the narrow inner border.

4 Using the white pearl cotton, make a tie in the centre of each striped square. To do this, take a small stitch, leaving a 2 in/5 cm loose end. Take another stitch over the top of the previous one and cut off the thread, leaving a 2 in/5 cm tail. Tie the two ends in a reef knot, then trim the ends level.

5 Trim the wadding and backing fabric in line with the pieced top. From the remaining border and binding fabric, cut six strips across the width of the fabric, 3 in/7.5 cm deep, cut two of these in half and rejoin one half piece to each of the remaining four strips.

6 Fold the binding strips in half lengthwise, right sides together, and press. Use to bind the edges with a double-fold binding with squared corners.

Butterfly Blue Throw

DESIGNED
BY
Sarah Wellfair

A wonderful selection of butterfly print fabrics make up this rotary cut, quick-pieced throw, which can easily be made in a weekend. It can be enlarged by making more blocks or by adding more borders.

Quilt assembly diagram

Finished size: 44$\frac{1}{2}$ x 53$\frac{1}{2}$ in/107 x 128 cm

Materials

All fabrics used in the quilt top are 45 in/115 cm wide, 100% cotton

For the block centres and binding: blue (A), 20 in/50 cm

For the block strips: blue and green print (B),

10 in/25 cm; blue and gold print (C), 20 in/50 cm

For the block strips and border: blue and green large print (D), 1$\frac{1}{3}$ yds/1.1 m

For the setting triangles: green print (E), 20 in/50 cm

Backing: 1$\frac{2}{3}$ yds/1.5 m, 45 in/115 cm wide

Wadding: lightweight, 1$\frac{2}{3}$ yds/1.5 m, 45 in/115 cm wide

Alternative colour schemes

1 Small florals with the cream contrast make the chevrons very bold.

2 Hand-dyed fabrics give a softer blend of colour.

3 The batiks give a very pretty block, and the chevrons fade together.

4 Blues give an icier look to the block.

Cutting

1 From fabric A, cut two strips, 2 in/5 cm deep, across the width of the fabric; cut five strips, 3 in/7.5 cm deep, across the width for the binding.

2 From fabric B, cut five strips, 2 in/5 cm deep, across the width of the fabric.

3 From fabric C, cut seven strips, 2 in/5 cm deep, across the width of the fabric.

4 From fabric D, cut ten strips, 2 in/5 cm deep, across the width of the fabric; cut five strips, 4½ in/11.5 cm deep, across the width.

5 From fabric E, cut four squares, 9¾ in/24.5 cm wide, then cross-cut into four along both diagonals to make quarter-square triangles for the sides – you will need fourteen in total. Cut two squares, 5⅛ in/13 cm wide, then cross-cut in half along one diagonal to make half-square triangles for the corners.

Stitching

1 Take one 2 in/5 cm deep strip of fabric A and one of fabric B, place right sides together and stitch along one long edge, taking a ¼ in/0.75 cm seam allowance. Press the seam towards fabric B. Repeat with a second set of fabrics A and B.

2 Cross-cut the strip units into 2 in/5 cm sections – 32 in total are needed (diagram 1).

diagram 1

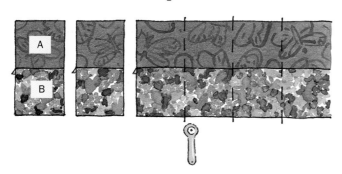

3 Take the three remaining strips of fabric B and cut into 32 pieces, 3½ in/8.5 cm long. Chain piece one short strip to the right-hand side of each of the 32 units made in step 2 (diagram 2).

diagram 2

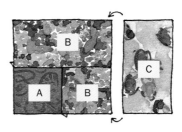

4 Take three strips of fabric C and cut into 32 pieces, 3½ in/8.5 cm long. Chain piece to the right-hand side of the units made in step 3 (diagram 3). Press the seams towards fabric C.

diagram 3

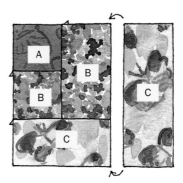

5 Take the remaining four strips of fabric C and cut 32 pieces, 5 in/12 cm long. Chain piece to the adjacent side of the units (diagram 4). Press as before.

diagram 4

6 Take the ten 2 in/5 cm strips of fabric D and cut 32 pieces, 5 in/12 cm long, and 32 pieces, $6^{1}/_{2}$ in/ 15.5 cm long. Chain piece in turn to the sides of the blocks following diagrams 5a and 5b. Press the seams towards fabric D. You should now have 32 blocks measuring $6^{1}/_{2}$ in/15.5 cm.

diagram 5a

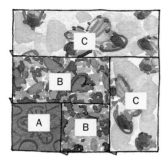

diagram 5b

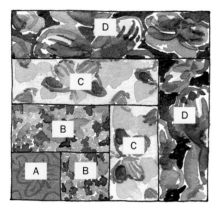

7 Following the quilt assembly diagram on page 76, lay out the blocks in diagonal rows together with setting triangles and corner triangles.

8 Stitch together in diagonal rows, then stitch the rows together.

Adding the borders

1 Measure the pieced top through the centre from top to bottom, then trim two of the $4^{1}/_{2}$ in/11.5 cm wide fabric D border strips to this measurement. Stitch to the sides of the pieced top.

2 Stitch the remaining three $4^{1}/_{2}$ in/11.5 cm wide fabric D border strips together into one long strip. Measure

the pieced top through the centre from side to side, then cut this long strip into two pieces to this measurement. Stitch to the top and bottom of the pieced top.

Finishing

1 Measure the pieced top, then add 2 in/5 cm to each side and cut the backing fabric and wadding to these measurements.

2 Spread the backing right side down on a flat surface, then smooth out the wadding and the pieced top, right side up, on top. Fasten together with safety pins or baste in a grid.

3 Using contrasting thread, quilt in a random pattern all over the design.

4 Join the binding strips into one length and use to make a double-fold mitred binding.

Love and Kisses Quilt

DESIGNED
BY
Jean Hunt

The inspiration for this quilt came from a unique fabric, which I made using small pieces bonded together. We are so lucky to have modern materials to hand when making a quilt – this one uses fusible web, and could be made from a large scrap bag, from fabric leftover from a quilt, or from a pack of fat quarters. It is a very good excuse for using all the decorative stitches on your sewing machine.

Quilt assembly diagram

Finished size: 41 x 53 in/102 x 132 cm

Materials

All fabrics used in the quilt top are 45 in/115 cm wide, 100% cotton

For the background of the squares and foundation fabric: white, 2 yds/2 m

For the crazy patchwork: nine fat quarters of toning fabrics, light medium and dark.

Fusible webbing: 3³/₄ yds/3.5 m, about 18 in/50 cm wide

For the binding: in a colour to match or slightly darker than the crazy patchwork colours, 20 in/50 cm

Backing: 1³/₄ yds/1.5 m

Wadding: 2 oz polyester, 44 x 56 in/107 x 137 cm

Stiff card

Tracing or freezer paper

White machine embroidery thread

Contrasting variegated machine quilting thread

Alternative colour schemes

1 Use blue and silver fabrics to make a Christmassy design.

2 Try a different appliqué shape, such as a flower pattern in greens.

3 Or a star pattern in golds and creams.

4 Or a pretty butterfly in pinks and purples to make a quilt for a child's bed.

Cutting

1 From the white fabric, cut 12 squares, 10$\frac{1}{2}$ in/26.5 cm wide, for the backing squares. The rest of the white material will be used as a foundation fabric for the crazy patchwork.

2 From the nine coloured fat quarters, cut random pieces, approximately 2–3 in/5–8 cm wide, for the crazy patchwork shapes, sashing and borders.

3 From the binding fabric, cut six strips, 2 in/5 cm deep, across the width of the fabric.

4 Enlarge the hearts and kisses templates below, then using the tracing or freezer paper, make six kisses and six hearts.

Templates
50% of actual size.
Set photocopier to 200% to enlarge to correct size

Stitching

1 Take the remaining white fabric, which should measure approximately 40 x 44 in/120 x 112 cm in length. Onto the right side of this, iron enough fusible web to cover the whole surface. Peel the paper backing off the fusible web.

2 Take the bags of coloured fabric, and with the fusible web surface towards you, start covering the surface with the crazy pieces, right side up, randomly, overlapping the edges very slightly. Iron in place, according to the manufacturer's instructions. Any leftovers will be used for the love and kisses blocks.

3 Using decorative stitches on your machine, and variegated thread, cover the raw edges of the crazy pieces with stitching. Tie the ends off neatly.

4 From this crazy patchwork fabric, cut five strips, 2$\frac{1}{2}$ in/6 cm deep, across the width, then cross-cut two of these into eight 10$\frac{1}{2}$ in/26.5 cm lengths for the sashing. Next, cut five strips, 3$\frac{1}{2}$ in/9 cm deep, across the width for the borders (diagram 1).

diagram 1

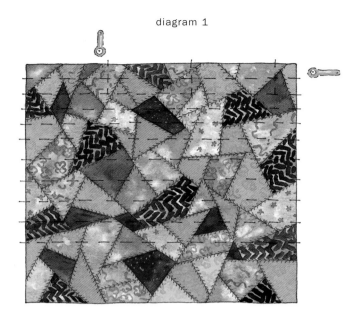

5 Take the remaining fusible web (approximately $1^{1}/_{2}$ yds/1.25 m) and the remaining bags of scraps. Lay the fusible web in front of you, rough side up. Cover the web with scraps as before, then put a spare piece of cloth on top and iron in place.

6 Turn the fabric over and, using the hearts and kisses templates, draw the shapes onto the smooth side of the web.

7 Cut out these shapes, peel off the paper backing and position each one onto the middle of one of the white $10^{1}/_{2}$ in/26.5 cm squares. This doesn't have to be completely accurate; it looks good if the crosses are offset slightly. Iron each one in position.

8 Using the decorative stitches on your machine, for example, herringbone or blanket stitch, cover the raw edges with stitching; also stitch around the outer edge of the shape with decorative stitching (diagram 2). Tie off any loose ends.

diagram 2

9 Following the quilt assembly diagram on page 82, lay out the blocks in four rows of three blocks, with sashing strips in between.

10 Stitch a short sashing strip between each block to form the columns of blocks. Press the seams towards the sashing strips, then stitch a long sashing strip between the columns. Press as before.

11 Join the five $3^{1}/_{2}$ in/9 cm border strips together into one length. To cover the joins, add a few pieces from your bags of crazy fabrics and add decorative stitching as before (diagram 3), then trim level with the edges.

diagram 3

12 Measure the pieced top through the centre from side to side, then cut two strips to this length. Stitch to the top and bottom of the quilt.

13 Measure the pieced top through the centre from top to bottom, then cut two strips to this length from the remaining border strip. Stitch to the sides. Press lightly.

Finishing

1 Spread the backing right side down on a flat surface, then smooth out the wadding and the patchwork top, right side up, on top. Fasten together with safety pins or baste in a grid.

2 Cover the white background of the blocks with vermicelli quilting. The quilt shown has also been quilted in-the-ditch around the blocks using the same variegated thread and using a walking foot, but this is optional.

3 Join the binding strips with diagonal seams to make a continuous length to fit all round the quilt and use to bind the edges with a double-fold binding, mitred at the corners.

Star Bright

DESIGNED
BY
Sarah
Wellfair

This is a simple two block quilt that is very quick and easy to make using quick piecing and rotary cutting techniques. The star shape is echoed in the star fabric used in the block corners and outer border.

Quilt assembly diagram

Finished size: 57 x 75 in/145 x 191 cm

Materials

All fabrics used in the quilt top are 45 in/115 cm wide, 100% cotton

For the stars and outer border squares: turquoise, 30 in/75 cm

For the stars and inner border: cream-on-cream, $1^{1}/_{2}$ yds/1.25 m

For the stars: pink, $1^{1}/_{4}$ yds/1 m

For the stars, inner border squares and outer border: purple, $1^{2}/_{3}$ yds/1.5 m

Backing: $3^{1}/_{3}$ yds/3 m

Binding: purple, 24 in/60 cm

Wadding: cotton, 60 x 80 in/150 x 200 cm

Alternative colour schemes

1 Pastel stars in a floral background look soft and pretty.

2 Two-tone stars can look very striking – shown here in black and white prints.

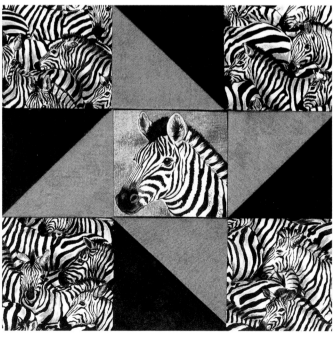

3 Using an animal print for the centre makes a lovely children's quilt.

4 A dark background with lighter stars works well; the directional print looks good for the corner blocks.

Cutting

1 From the turquoise, cut seven strips, 3½ in/9 cm deep, across the width of the fabric; cut four 4½in/11.5 cm squares for the outer border.

2 From the cream, cut eight strips, 3½ in/9 cm deep, across the width of the fabric; cut four strips, 3⅞ in/10 cm deep, across the width, then cross-cut into 36, 3⅞ in/10 cm squares. Discard leftover strips.

3 From the pink, cut four strips, 3⅞ in/10 cm deep, across the width of the fabric, then cross-cut into 36, 3⅞ in/10 cm squares; cut two strips, 3½ in/9 cm deep, across the width, then cross-cut these into 18, 3½ in/9 cm squares. Cut six strips, 2½ in/6 cm deep, across the width for the inner border.

4 From the purple, cut six strips, 3½ in/9 cm deep, across the width of the fabric, then cross-cut these into 72, 3½ in/9 cm squares; cut four, 2½ in/6 cm squares for the inner border. Cut seven strips, 4½ in/11.5 cm deep, across the width for the outer border. Discard left-over strips.

5 From the binding fabric, cut seven strips, 3 in/7.5 cm deep, across the width of the fabric.

Stitching

1 Take two turquoise 3½ in/9 cm strips and one cream 3½ in/9 cm strip and stitch together down the long sides with the cream strip in the centre, taking a ¼ in/0.75 cm seam allowance. Press the seams towards the turquoise. Repeat to make another strip.

2 Cross-cut these units into 17, 3½ in/9 cm strips (diagram 1).

diagram 1

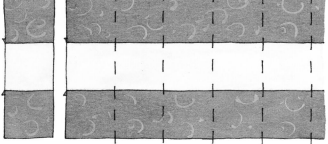

3 Take two cream 3½ in/9 cm strips and one turquoise 3½ in/9 cm strip and stitch together down the long sides with the turquoise strip in the centre, taking a ¼ in/0.75 cm seam allowance. Press the seams towards the turquoise. Repeat to make two more strips.

4 Cross-cut these units into 34, 3½ in/9 cm strips (diagram 2).

diagram 2

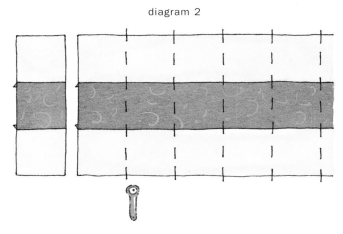

5 Place one strip cut in step 2 right sides together with one strip cut in step 4. Stitch, taking the usual seam allowance, and press seam to one side. Stitch a second unit cut in step 4 to the other side of the unit cut in step 2 to make a nine-patch block (diagram 3). Repeat to make a total of 17 blocks.

diagram 3

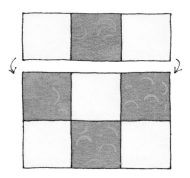

6 Take the pink and the cream 3⅞ in/10 cm squares and place right sides together in pairs with the cream squares uppermost. Draw a diagonal line from corner to corner on the cream, then stitch ¼ in/0.75 cm on either side of the marked line. Cut in half along the marked line, open out and press the seams towards the pink.

7 Following diagram 4, lay out the purple and pink squares, interspersed with the half-triangle squares, to make the star block.

diagram 4

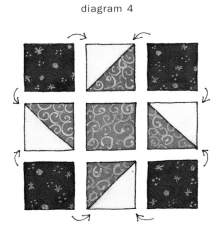

8 Stitch the squares together in rows, then stitch the rows together. Repeat to make a total of 18 blocks.

9 Following the quilt assembly diagram on page 88, lay out the blocks, alternating the nine-patch with the star blocks, in seven rows of five blocks.

10 Stitch the blocks together in rows, then stitch the rows together.

Adding the borders

1 Stitch three of the pink $2^{1}/_{2}$ in/6 cm wide border strips together into one long strip. Measure the pieced top through the centre from side to side, then cut the long strip into two pieces to this measurement. Stitch to the top and bottom of the pieced top. Press the seams towards the borders.

2 Stitch the remaining three pink $2^{1}/_{2}$ in/6 cm wide border strips together into one long strip. Measure the pieced top through the centre from top to bottom excluding the borders just added, add $^{1}/_{2}$ in/1.5 cm, then cut the long strip into two pieces to this measurement. Stitch a purple $2^{1}/_{2}$ in/6 cm square at either end of each of these two strips, then stitch to either side of the pieced top to complete the inner border. Press as before.

3 Repeat steps 1 and 2 but using the seven $4^{1}/_{2}$ in/11.5 cm purple outer border strips and the four $4^{1}/_{2}$ in/11.5 cm turquoise squares. You will need to join the purple border strips into one long length, then trim into the four separate lengths once the pieced top has been measured. Press the seams towards the purple borders.

Finishing

1 Cut the backing fabric in two crosswise, trim off the selvages and join together down one long side. Trim an even amount off both long sides to make a piece measuring 60 x 80 in/150 x 200 cm.

2 Spread the backing right side down on a flat surface, then smooth out the wadding and the pieced top, right side up, on top. Fasten together with safety pins or baste in a grid.

3 Quilt in a random pattern on the cream, quilt free motion stars in the borders and quilt free motion swirls on the pink stars.

4 Trim the excess wadding and backing level with the pieced top.

5 Stitch the binding strips into one long length, then fold in half, wrong sides together lengthwise, and press.

6 Measure the quilt through the centre from top to bottom, then cut two binding strips to this length. Stitch to the sides of the pieced top, right sides together and matching raw edges, taking a $^{1}/_{2}$ in/1.5 cm seam allowance. Flip the binding to the reverse of the quilt and slip stitch in place along the stitching line.

7 Measure the pieced top through the centre from side to side, add $1^{1}/_{2}$ in/4 cm to this measurement, then cut two more binding strips to this length. Stitch to the top and bottom of the quilt, leaving $^{3}/_{4}$ in/2 cm over at either end. Turn in the ends of binding, flip to the back and slip stitch in place as before.

Blue and White Ohio Stars Bed Quilt

DESIGNED
BY
Alison Wood

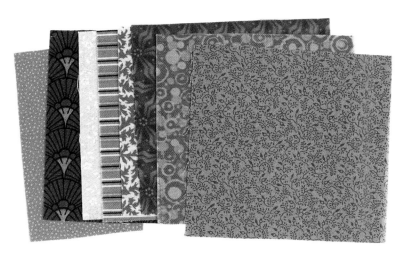

A galaxy of blue stars sparkles on this single bed quilt, which is edged with a "Folded Ribbon" border. A quick method used for the Ohio Stars helps to achieve accurate star points. The border is a little more complicated to sew, but well worth the extra time. A selection of blue fabrics has been used against a unifying white-on-white floral sprig for the background.

Quilt assembly diagram

Finished size: 70 in x 88 in/178 x 224 cm

Materials

All fabrics used in the quilt are 45 in/115 cm wide, 100% cotton.

For the background and borders: white-on-white floral sprig, 6$\frac{1}{4}$ yds/6.10 m (ask for this in two pieces: 3$\frac{3}{4}$ yds/3.85 m for the star backgrounds and 2$\frac{1}{2}$ yds/2.25 m for the borders and binding – it is too difficult to cut the pieces from one long length)

Binding: 20 in/50 cm (if a different colour from background fabric is used, see the note opposite)

For the stars: various small floral blue prints, 2 yds/1.75 m or equivalent in scraps (as a rough guide, a metric fat quarter will yield eight stars, and you will need a total of 48 stars)

For the folded ribbon border: dark blue, 10 in/25 cm; medium blue, 1 yd/90 cm

Backing: 5 yds/4.75 m of 45 in/115 cm wide fabric

Wadding: lightweight, 74 in x 92 in/188 cm x 233 cm

NOTE

For the binding, I used the same fabric as the background so that it would not take attention away from the star blocks and ribbon border. If you do the same, you will not need any extra binding fabric as you can cut the binding from the amount allowed for the plain borders.

Alternative colour schemes

1 A very different look would be obtained by using dramatic batiks.

2 The floral pink and yellow fabrics make a cheerful design.

3 Christmas stars twinkling with gold.

4 A selection from my stash of scrap fabrics gives a country look.

Cutting

1 From the 2¹⁄₂ yds/2.25 m piece of white fabric, cut eight strips, 3¹⁄₂ in/9 cm wide, down the length of the fabric for the borders. These will be trimmed to fit. Cut four 2¹⁄₂ in/6 cm strips, also from the length of the fabric, for the binding. (If you are using a different-coloured binding, cut eight 2¹⁄₂ in/6 cm strips from the width of the binding fabric.)

2 From the remaining piece of white fabric, cut ten strips, 4¹⁄₄ in/11 cm deep, across the width and cross-cut these into 96 squares for the star points. Cut 16 strips, 3¹⁄₂ in/9 cm deep, across the width and cross-cut into 192 squares for the corners of the star blocks. Cut six strips, 3¹⁄₂ in/9 cm deep, across the width for the folded ribbon border. Cut two 4¹⁄₄ in/11 cm squares and cut these in half diagonally for the four corner triangles.

NOTE

Cutting from the length of the fabric avoids joins. There is also less stretch in the fabric, which is helpful when attaching long, narrow borders such as these, especially when stitching to a bias edge.

3 From each of the fabrics chosen for the stars, cut strips, 4¹⁄₄ in/11 cm deep, across the width of the fabric and cross-cut these into squares. You will need a total of 96 squares for the star points. Cut 48, 3¹⁄₂ in/9 cm squares for the star centres.

4 From the dark blue ribbon border fabric, cut three strips, 2¹⁄₂ in/6 cm deep, across the width.

5 From the medium blue ribbon border fabric, cut ten strips, 2¹⁄₂ in/6 cm deep, across the width and cross-cut nine of these strips into 44, 8 in/20 cm lengths (each strip will yield five, so you will have one length extra), plus four 10 in/26 cm lengths from the remaining strip for the corners.

Stitching

1 Draw a diagonal line with a pencil across the wrong side of each of the 96 white 4¹⁄₄ in/11 cm squares, which will form the background to the star points.

2 Take one blue 4¹⁄₄ in/11 cm square and put it right sides together with one of the white squares you have just marked. Stitch a seam line ¹⁄₄ in/0.75 cm away on either side of the drawn line (diagram 1). Repeat with the remaining 95 pairs of squares. Chain piecing will save time and thread.

diagram 1

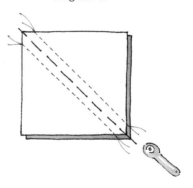

3 Cut the threads between the squares. Press each stitched pair of squares flat to set the seams, then cut along the drawn diagonal line. Press the seams towards the darker fabric.

4 Take half of the units and, on the wrong side, draw a diagonal line in the opposite direction from the seam. Take one unmarked unit and put it right sides together with a marked unit, so that the white half of one unit is on top of the blue half of the other and vice versa. Stitch a ¹⁄₄ in/0.75 cm seam on either side of the drawn diagonal (diagram 2).

diagram 2

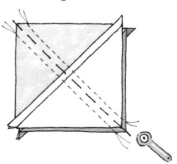

5 Repeat with all the remaining pairs of half square units, then press each pair flat to set the seams before cutting along the drawn diagonal line.

6 Press each stitched unit open. You should have 192 quarter square units, four for each star block in the quilt, and each should measure $3^{1}/_{2}$ in/9 cm. Trim off the "ears".

7 Stitch two quarter square units to one matching blue $3^{1}/_{2}$ in/9 cm square and stitch two white background $3^{1}/_{2}$ in/9 cm squares to either side of two more quarter square units as shown in diagram 3. Press seam allowances towards the whole squares.

diagram 3

8 Join the three rows of units together to make one star block. Press the seam allowances towards the centre square. Repeat to make a total of 48 star blocks.

9 When all the blocks have been pieced, stitch the blocks together into eight rows of six blocks as shown in the quilt assembly plan on page 94. Press the seams between the blocks in opposite directions for alternate rows.

10 When all the rows have been joined, press the top lightly.

Adding the borders

1 To add the inner plain white borders, measure the pieced top through the centre from top to bottom and trim two of the white $3^{1}/_{2}$ in/9 cm border strips to this length. Pin and stitch to the sides of the pieced top. Press the seam allowances towards the borders. Measure the pieced top through the centre from side to side, then trim two more strips to this measurement. Stitch to the top and bottom and press as before.

2 To make the folded ribbon border, stitch one dark blue $2^{1}/_{2}$ in/6 cm wide strip between two white background $3^{1}/_{2}$ in/9 cm strips along the long sides, taking a $^{1}/_{4}$ in/0.75 cm seam allowance and being careful not to stretch and curve the strips as you are sewing. Repeat with the remaining two dark blue strips and four white strips. Press the seam allowances towards the dark blue fabric.

3 Cross-cut the three strip sets into 46 rectangles, $2^{1}/_{2}$ in/6 cm wide (diagram 4).

diagram 4

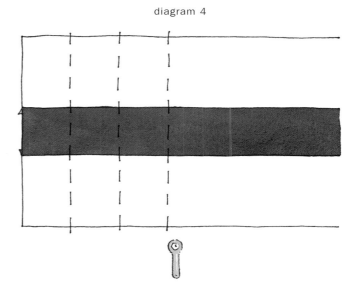

4 Stitch one of these rectangles to one medium blue
$2^{1}/_{2}$ x 8 in/6 x 20 cm rectangle as follows: mark a
crease halfway down the white top part of the rectangle
and line up the top of the medium blue strip with this
crease mark, right sides together (diagram 5). Stitch
together. Stitch the remaining rectangles together in
pairs with half of the medium blue strips to the right-
hand edge of the slice, and half to the left-hand edge.
You will have 22 of each and two spare slices. Press
towards the medium blue strip

diagram 5

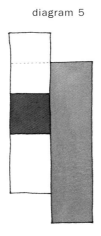

5 Stitch six of the left-handed units together in a
staggered row, lining up the bottom of the medium blue
strip so that it is $^{1}/_{4}$ in/0.75 cm beyond the bottom of
the adjoining dark blue square (diagram 6a). Press the
seams towards the medium blue strips. Repeat with six
of the right-handed units (6b).

diagram 6

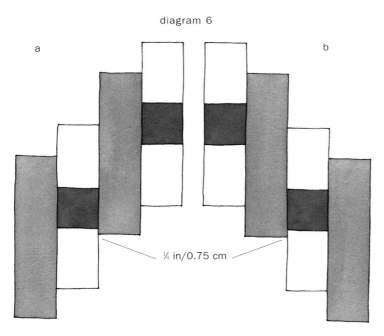

a   b

$^{1}/_{4}$ in/0.75 cm

6 Trim away the ends of the strips in a straight line,
taking care to ensure that there is a $^{1}/_{4}$ in/0.75 cm
seam allowance beyond the points of the dark blue
squares (diagram 7).

diagram 7

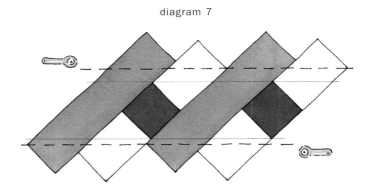

7 Study the quilt assembly plan and you will see that
there are two different ways of reversing the direction of
the folded ribbon, so as to keep the corners of the quilt
the same. Depending on the size of your patchwork top,
you may find that one or the other method will help your
border fit better. Instructions for both methods follow.

8 Pin the border strips along one side of the patchwork
top, starting at each end and handling the strips with
care, as these are now all cut bias edges. Decide on the
most suitable method of joining the strips at the mid-
point. If your medium blue strips are close enough to
overlap (as at the top and bottom of this quilt), piece in
a small background triangle cut to fit the space available
(mine was cut from a $2^{1}/_{2}$ in/6 cm square).

9 If your medium blue strips only just meet, however
(as at the sides of this quilt), take one of the spare rectangles and unpick the top background piece, joining it
onto the other side of the dark blue square so that the
unit can be trimmed into a triangle to fit the space available (diagram 8). Whichever treatment is chosen, you
must use the same method on the opposite border,
although you can use different methods for the sides
and top and bottom, as in the quilt photographed.

diagram 8

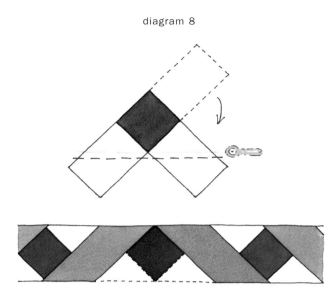

10 Now join the strip units to make the other side border, using six right-handed and six left-handed units, and press and trim as before. When stitching the border strips to the quilt, check the quilt assembly diagram to make sure that the ribbon is going in the right direction, leaving the corners open for the longer strips to be added last. Press the seam allowances towards the inner plain border.

NOTE

If you find you are having difficulty making the folded ribbon border fit, you may be able to reduce the width of the inner plain border, or add a narrow "filler" strip, to bring the top up to the size you need.

11 Join the remaining strip units and attach them to the top and bottom. This time, there will only be five right-handed and five left-handed units for each.

12 Take the four 10 in/26 cm medium blue strips and stitch them diagonally across the corners to complete the ribbon. Press the seam allowance towards the ribbon and trim to square off the corners. Add the white corner triangles and press the seam allowance towards the ribbon.

13 Finally, attach the outer plain borders to the sides first and then to the top and bottom, measuring through the middle of the quilt as before, and taking particular care when stitching them in place that you do not stretch the bias edges of the folded ribbon border. Press towards the outer edges of the quilt top.

Finishing

1 Measure the completed quilt top and cut and piece the backing to fit with at least 2 in/5 cm all round. If you are joining the backing, don't forget to cut off the selvages as these are very tightly woven and can cause distortion in the quilt. Press the seam open.

2 Spread the backing right side down on a flat surface, then smooth out the wadding and the patchwork top, right side up, on top. Fasten together with safety pins or baste in a grid.

3 Mark the top with the desired quilting design. I quilted in-the-ditch along the seam lines between the blocks, then added additional straight lines by quilting in-the-ditch along the seams on either side of the star centres. Next, I quilted long diagonal lines in-the-ditch through the star point units: the continuation of the diagonal lines forms a secondary square on point quilting pattern between the stars. These diagonals were marked with a plastic tool called a Hera marker and a long ruler; the marker makes an indentation in the layered quilt that shows up well on light-coloured fabric. Finally, I quilted the plain borders $1/4$ in/0.75 cm in from the seam lines.

4 Join the binding strips with diagonal seams to make a continuous length to fit all round the quilt and use to bind the edges with a double-fold binding, mitred at the corners.

Summer Fields Bed Quilt

DESIGNED
BY
Rita
Whitehorn

The fresh pink, green and white fabrics remind me of strawberries and the curvy star shape of buttercups in the fields in summertime. The quilt is simply pieced with four-patch blocks and alternating plain squares with an appliquéed star.

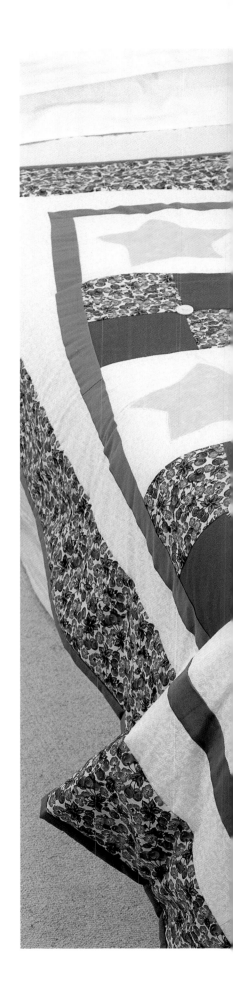

100

Quilt assembly diagram

Finished size: 73 x 73 in/183 x 183 cm

Materials

All fabrics used in the quilt top are 45 in/115 cm wide, 100% cotton

For the four-patch blocks and outer border: pink and green patterned fabric, 3 yds/3 m

For the four-patch blocks: pink, 20in/50 cm

For the four-patch blocks, inner border and binding: green, 1¼ yds/1.1 m

For the alternate blocks and middle border: white, 3 yds/3 m

For the stars: yellow, 20 in/50 cm

Backing: 4¼ yds/4 m

Fusible web: 30 in/75 cm

Wadding: 77 x 77 in/193 x 193 cm

Yellow quilting thread

Thread to match binding and star

Template plastic

12 buttons

Alternative colour schemes

1 A fresh aqua and pink floral fabric produces a sunny design.

2 A larger floral fabric will become the dominant fabric, especially if matched with softer plain fabrics.

3 Lilacs, greens and blues matched with blue stars produce a calming colour scheme.

4 The quilt design could also be made with a child's novelty fabric in lively colours.

Cutting

1 From the pink and green patterned fabric, cut three strips, $5^{1/2}$ in/14 cm deep, across the width of the fabric. Cut four strips, $6^{1/2}$ in/16.5 cm wide, from down the length for the outer border.

2 From the pink fabric, cut two strips, $5^{1/2}$ in/14 cm deep, across the width of the fabric.

3 From the green fabric, cut one strip, $5^{1/2}$ in/14 cm deep, across the width of the fabric; cut six strips, 3 in/7.5 cm deep, across width for the binding; cut six strips, 2 in/5 cm deep, across the width for the inner border.

4 From the white fabric, cut 13, $10^{1/2}$ in/26.5 cm squares. Cut four strips, $3^{1/2}$ in/9 cm wide, from down the length for the middle border.

5 Using the template plastic, enlarge and make a star template from the design opposite.

6 Cut the backing fabric in half crosswise.

Stitching

1 Place one patterned and one pink $5^{1/2}$ in/14 cm strip right sides together and stitch along one long side, taking a $^{1/4}$ in/0.75 cm seam (diagram 1). Press towards the darker fabric. Repeat with the remaining two patterned and pink strips.

diagram 1

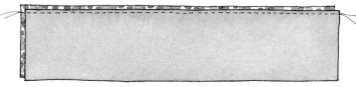

2 Place one patterned and one green $5^{1/2}$ in/14 cm strip right sides together and stitch along one long side, taking a $^{1/4}$ in/0.75 cm seam. Press towards the darker fabric.

3 Trim the selvage edges from all of the strips, then sub-cut into $5^{1/2}$ in/14 cm sections. Reversing the colour sequence, stitch two pairs of these sections together to

Template

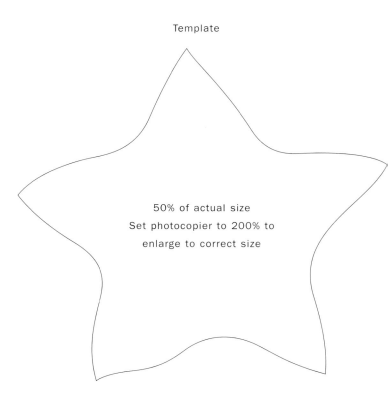

50% of actual size
Set photocopier to 200% to
enlarge to correct size

make four-patch squares (diagram 2). You will need a total of eight pink and patterned squares and four green and patterned squares.

diagram 2

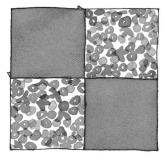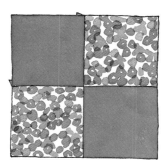

4 Iron the fusible web onto the wrong side of the yellow fabric, then using the template, trace the star shape onto the backing paper 13 times. Cut out the stars. Peel off the paper backing and position the stars in the middle of each of the white $10^{1/2}$ in/26.5 cm squares. Iron in place following the instructions on the fusible web for the heat setting.

5 Using a decorative stitch, stitch all around each star, starting on a long side (not a point). Stitch a small section at a time. When reaching a point of the star, leave the needle in the down position and lift the machine foot and pivot the work slightly to re-align it to stitch the next section. When the whole star has been sewn, run over a few stitches to lock the thread, drawing the ends through to back of work and secure.

6 Following the quilt assembly diagram on page 102, arrange the four-patch squares and star squares in five rows of five squares. Mark each row on the back of a white square lightly in pencil to keep rows in sequence.

7 Stitch the squares in each row together and press the seams towards the darker squares. Then stitch the rows together, pressing the seams all in the same direction.

Adding the borders

1 To add the inner border, cut two of the 2 in/5 cm green strips in half and stitch one to each of the remaining four green strips. Measure the pieced top through the centre from top to bottom, then trim two of the strips to this measurement. Stitch to the sides of the quilt. Press towards the border. Measure the pieced top through the centre from side to side, then trim the remaining two strips to this measurement. Pin and stitch to the top and bottom and press as before.

2 To add the middle border, measure the pieced top through the centre from top to bottom, then trim two of the strips to this measurement. Stitch to the sides of the quilt. Press towards the inner border. Measure the pieced top through the centre from side to side, then trim the remaining two strips to this measurement. Pin and stitch to the top and bottom and press as before.

3 To add the outer border, measure the pieced top through the centre from top to bottom, then trim two of the strips to this measurement. Stitch to the sides of the quilt. Press towards the outer border. Measure the pieced top through the centre from side to side, then trim the remaining two strips to this measurement. Pin and stitch to the top and bottom and press as before.

4 To make the backing, place the two rectangles right sides together and stitch down the longer side. Press the seam to one side, then trim an even amount off both sides to make a square, 77 x 77 in/193 x 193 cm.

5 Spread the backing right side down on a flat surface, then smooth out the wadding and the patchwork top, right side up, on top. Fasten together with safety pins or baste in a grid.

6 Machine quilt round the stars, then using white embroidery thread, stitch buttons in the middle of each four-patch square, leaving a length of thread to tie in the centre of the button. Trim to the length required (diagram 3).

diagram 3

7 Stitch the eight 3 in/7.5 cm green binding strips together in pairs to make four long strips. Fold the strips in half lengthwise, right sides together, and press. Place one strip along one side of the quilt, aligning the raw edges, trim to fit and stitch taking the usual seam allowance. Fold to the back of the quilt and hem stitch in place along the stitching line. Repeat on the opposite side.

8 For the remaining two sides, stitch the strips to the quilt in the same way, but before folding to the back trim the strips so that they are $\frac{1}{4}$ in/0.75 cm longer than the quilt at each end. Fold in the short overlap, then fold the binding to the back and hem stitch in place.

Blue and White Strippy

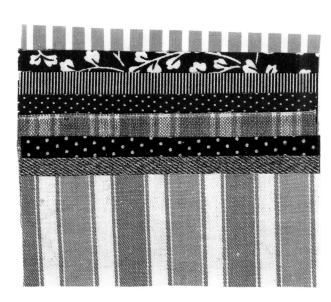

DESIGNED
BY
Jill Leman

This striped quilt is a very satisfying way of recycling a selection of old clothes – a favourite shirt, a summer frock and a much loved pair of denim jeans – to make a wonderfully comfortable bed cover that contains many memories . It was inspired by the ingenuity of early American quilts, which showed that something as necessary as a bed covering can also be beautiful.

Quilt assembly diagram

Finished size: 72 x 84 in/183 x 214 cm

Materials

Scrap fabrics: collect together suitable blue and blue and white materials, such as old shirts, pyjamas, cotton dresses and denim jeans. As a guide, you can get roughly two strips from one pair of jeans or pyjamas and one strip from a shirt

Backing: soft sheeting or cotton, $4^{1}/_{4}$ yds/4 m

Wadding: a piece, 76 x 88 in/193 x 224 cm (If the wadding needs to be joined to make a piece of this size, stitch together by hand using herringbone stitches. See page 13)

Binding: blue, $1^{1}/_{2}$ yds/1.25 m

Alternative colour schemes

1 Paisley fine wool and checks, with a fine spotted border, make a richly coloured quilt for winter.

2 Summer dresses and other fine cotton prints in pinks and ochres can be recycled for this design.

3 This striped quilt in blue and white makes me think of beach houses and seaside holidays all year round.

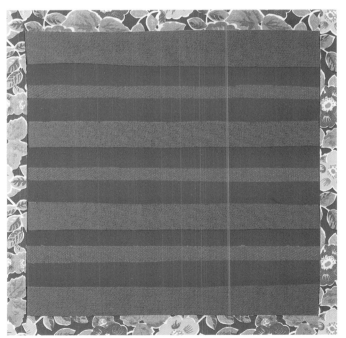

4 Vibrant pinks, reds and greens inspired by abstract art-works, such as Amish quilts – though its jazzy floral border makes it more "Pop Art" than they would approve.

Cutting

1 Cut off any sleeves, unpick the seams and iron flat. Cut off any collars. Cut as many strips as possible from each garment, either 3$\frac{1}{2}$ or 4 in/9 or 10 cm wide – keep to the same width for each individual garment (diagram 1). The aim is to join strips from each garment together to make a length, 84 in/214 cm long.

diagram 1

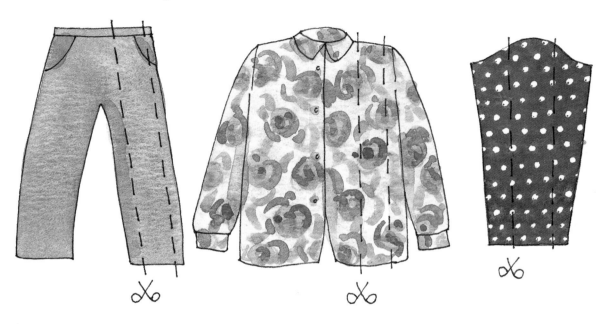

2 From the blue binding fabric, cut seven strips, 7$\frac{1}{2}$ in/17.5 cm deep, across the width of the fabric.

3 Cut the backing fabric in half crosswise.

Stitching

1 Join the strips cut from the same garment together into lengths, 84 in/214 cm long, and press the seams to one side (diagram 2). You will need approximately 22 strips.

diagram 2

2 Lay the strips out on the floor or on the bed and decide on the arrangement you like the best.

3 When you have decided on an arrangement that looks good, join the strips, right sides together, along the long edges, taking a $\frac{1}{4}$ in/0.75 cm seam (diagram 3). Press the seams open. Trim the side edges to straighten them.

diagram 3

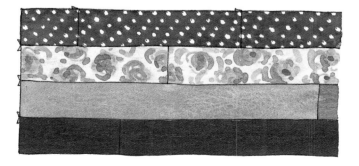

4 Stitch the two pieces of backing fabric together down one long edge, taking a $\frac{1}{2}$ in/1.5 cm seam. Press the seam open.

Finishing

1 Spread the backing right side down on a flat surface, then smooth out the wadding and the pieced top, right side up, on top. Fasten together with safety pins or baste in a grid.

2 Machine quilt along the seam lines between the strips – you can do this from each end of the quilt, rolling it as you go to fit under the arm of your sewing machine. You could also quilt a line along the middle of each strip for a more quilted look, as I did.

3 Trim the edges of the backing and wadding level with the pieced top.

4 Join the binding strips into one length and use to make a double-fold mitred binding.

111

Dreaming in Colour

DESIGNED
BY
Sarah Wellfair

I have always been tempted by lovely fat quarter bundles, so I decided to make a fat quarter quilt that would use up some of the packs I have in my fabric collection. This quilt could be made much bigger by using two bundles.

Quilt assembly diagram

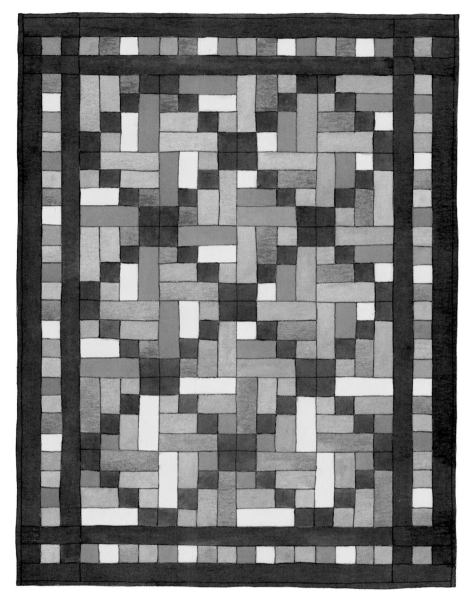

Finished size: 44$\frac{1}{2}$ x 60$\frac{1}{2}$ in/101 x 137 cm

Materials

All fabrics used in the quilt top are 45 in/115 cm wide, 100% cotton

Bright fabrics: 6 pieces, 19 x 22 in or 6 metric fat quarters (I have used blue, green and turquoise on one side of the block and orange, yellow and red on the other side)

Dark contrast: 1$\frac{1}{4}$ yds/1 m

Binding: 20 in/50 cm

Backing: 48$\frac{1}{2}$ x 64$\frac{1}{2}$ in/111 x 147 cm

Wadding: lightweight, 48$\frac{1}{2}$ x 64$\frac{1}{2}$ in/111 x 147 cm

Cutting

1 From each of the fat quarters cut the following:
one strip, 2$\frac{1}{2}$ x 22 in/6 x 56 cm;
one strip, 4$\frac{1}{2}$ x 22 in/11.5 x 56 cm;
one strip, 6$\frac{1}{2}$ x 22 in/16 x 56 cm

2 From the dark contrast fabric, cut six strips, 2$\frac{1}{2}$ in/ 6 cm deep, across the width of the fabric, then cut them in half to give 12 strips, 2$\frac{1}{2}$ x 22 in/6 x 56 cm.

3 From the binding fabric, cut five strips, 3 in/7.5 cm deep, across the width of the fabric.

Alternative colour schemes

1 Soft florals give a country-cottage look.

2 Flowers and dragonflies in yellow and lilac make a lovely children's quilt.

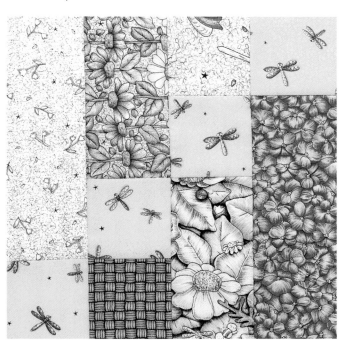

3 Dark reds and blues with a beige contrast create a country look.

4 Soft pastels with a dark contrast accentuate the diamonds created by the diagonal lines of squares.

Stitching

There are three different block colour combinations as shown in diagram 1.

diagram 1

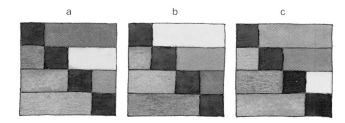

1 To make the first block, take one dark contrast strip and place it right sides together with one $6^{1}/_{2}$ in/16 cm red strip, aligning raw edges. Stitch down one long side, taking a $^{1}/_{4}$ in/0.75 cm seam allowance. Press towards the dark fabric.

2 Next, take another dark contrast strip, a blue $2^{1}/_{2}$ in/6 cm strip and a yellow $4^{1}/_{2}$ in/11.5 cm strip. Stitch together with the dark fabric in the middle. Press the seams towards the dark fabric.

3 Take another dark contrast strip, a green $4^{1}/_{2}$ in/11.5 cm strip and an orange $2^{1}/_{2}$ in/6 cm strip. Stitch together with the dark fabric in the middle. Press the seams towards the dark fabric.

4 Take another dark strip and a $6^{1}/_{2}$ in/16 cm turquoise strip. Stitch together down one long side. You should now have four pieced panels, as shown in diagram 2.

diagram 2

5 Cross-cut eight strips across each panel, $2^{1}/_{2}$ in/6 cm wide. Stitch the strips together in sets of four, as shown in diagram 1a to form eight blocks.

6 To make the second set of eight blocks (diagram 1b), work as steps 1 to 5 but piece the strips as follows: one dark strip to one $6^{1}/_{2}$ in/16 cm yellow; one dark strip between one $2^{1}/_{2}$ in/6 cm green and one $4^{1}/_{2}$ in/11.5 cm orange; one dark strip between one $4^{1}/_{2}$ in/11.5 cm turquoise and one $2^{1}/_{2}$ in/6 cm red; one dark strip and one $6^{1}/_{2}$ in/16 cm blue strip.

7 To make the third set of eight blocks (diagram 1c), work as steps 1 to 5 but piece strips as follows: one dark strip and one $6^{1}/_{2}$ in/16 cm orange; one dark strip between one $2^{1}/_{2}$ in/6 cm turquoise and one $4^{1}/_{2}$ in/11.5 cm red; one dark strip between one $4^{1}/_{2}$ in/11.5 cm blue and one $2^{1}/_{2}$ in/6 cm yellow; one dark strip to one $6^{1}/_{2}$ in/16 cm green.

8 Following the quilt assembly diagram on page 114, lay out the blocks in six rows of four blocks. Stitch together first in rows, then stitch the rows together.

Adding the borders

1 Take the remaining six fat quarter fabrics and cut one $2^{1}/_{2}$ x 22 in/6 x 56 cm strip from each. Stitch the strips together along the long sides in your chosen sequence, pressing the seams all in the same direction.

2 Cross-cut this stitched panel into eight $2^{1}/_{2}$ in/6 cm strips. Stitch four of these strips together to make one long strip. Repeat with the remaining four strips.

3 From the dark fabric, cut five strips $2^{1}/_{2}$ in/6 cm deep across the width of the fabric. Cut one strip into four equal pieces, then join one of these pieces to each of the remaining four strips. Take two of these strips and stitch one to either side of the multi-coloured strip (diagram 3). Trim level with the coloured squares. Press the seams towards the dark strips. Repeat with the two other dark strips.

diagram 3

4 Stitch one of these border units to each side of the pieced top.

5 Choose four of the remaining fat quarter colours and cut one $2\frac{1}{2}$ x 22 in/6 x 56 cm strip from each. Stitch together as described in step 1, then cross-cut into eight $2\frac{1}{2}$ in/6 cm sections as before. Stitch four of these strips together to make one long strip. Repeat with the remaining four strips.

6 From the dark fabric, cut four more strips, $2\frac{1}{2}$ in/ 6 cm deep, across the width of the fabric. Stitch to either side of the multi-coloured strips to make the top and bottom borders. Trim level and press the seams towards the darker strips.

7 To make the corner blocks, take the remaining two fat quarter colours and cut two $2\frac{1}{2}$ in/6 cm squares from each. From the dark fabric, cut eight $2\frac{1}{2}$ in/6 cm squares and eight pieces, $2\frac{1}{2}$ x $6\frac{1}{2}$ in/6 x 15 cm.

8 Stitch a dark square on either side of each of the four bright squares, taking the usual seam allowance, then stitch one dark strip on either side of this unit (diagram 4).

diagram 4

9 Stitch this pieced square to either end of the top and bottom border strips (diagram 5).

diagram 5

10 Stitch the top and bottom borders to the pieced top, matching corners carefully.

Finishing

1 Give the pieced top a final pressing and measure the sides, then cut the wadding and backing 2 in/5cm bigger all round than the pieced top.

2 Spread the backing right side down on a flat surface, then smooth out the wadding and the pieced top, right side up, on top. Fasten together with safety pins or baste in a grid.

3 Quilt as desired. I have free motion quilted with hearts, using a purple silky metallic thread and a metallic needle in my machine.

4 Trim the excess wadding and backing level with the pieced top.

5 Join the binding strips into one long length. Fold in half, wrong sides together lengthwise, and press.

6 Measure the quilt through the centre from top to bottom, then cut two strips to this length. Stitch to the sides of the pieced top, right sides together and matching raw edges, taking a $\frac{1}{2}$ in/1.5 cm seam allowance. Flip the binding to the reverse of the quilt and slip-stitch in place along the stitching line.

7 Measure the pieced top through the centre from side to side, add $1\frac{1}{2}$ in/4 cm to this measurement, then cut two more binding strips to this length. Stitch to the top and bottom of the quilt, leaving $\frac{3}{4}$ in/2 cm over at either end. Turn in the ends of binding, flip to the back and slip-stitch in place as before.

Waterwheel Bed Quilt

DESIGNED
BY
Mary
O'Riordan

The "Waterwheel" block is also known as "Tessellating Stars". It is a great project for quick cutting, as it only requires rectangles in two sizes. The blocks are really easy to make and work well whether you are using a multitude of scraps or a more restricted colour scheme.

Quilt assembly diagram

Finished size: 45 x 60 in/128 x 170 cm

Materials

All fabrics used in the quilt top are 45 in/115 cm wide, 100% cotton

For the background: white calico, 2 yds/1.75 m

For the "wheels" and borders: 16 fat eighths (10 x 22 in/ 23 x 56 cm) in a selection of pastel florals or fabric scraps to total 2¹/₂ yds/2.25 m

Binding: striped fabric or bright print, 20 in/50 cm

Backing: 2³/₄ yds/2.6 m

Wadding: 50 x 65 in/140 x 182 cm

Alternative colour schemes

1 Restrict yourself to leftovers from your scrap basket and sort them into lights and darks to produce an old-fashioned patchwork.

2 Flannels are a good choice for a cosy winter warmer in subdued colours.

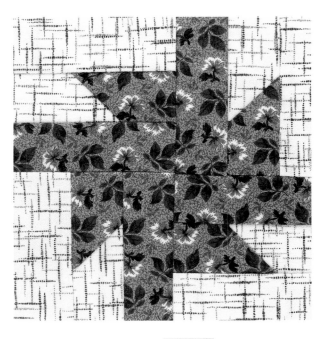

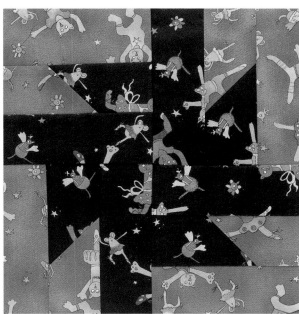

3 Use bold novelty prints to achieve a dramatic effect.

4 For a two-colour quilt, indigo on white is always a satisfying combination.

Cutting

1 From the white background fabric, cut 25 strips, 2 in/5.5 cm deep, across the width of the fabric and cross-cut into 120 rectangles measuring 2 x 5 in/ 5.5 x 13.5 cm and 120 rectangles measuring 2 x 3½ in/5.5 x 8.75 cm.

2 From the prints, cut 2 in/5.5 cm wide strips and cross-cut to produce 120 rectangles measuring 2 x 5 in/ 5.5 x 13.5 cm and 120 rectangles 2 x 3½ in/ 5.5 x 8.75 cm. Reserve the leftover fabric for the top and bottom borders.

3 For the binding, cut six strips, 2½ in/6.5 cm deep, across the width of the fabric.

Stitching

1 To make one block, line up the short side of a 2 x 3½ in/5.5 x 8.75 cm white background rectangle with the long side of the print rectangle of the same size, then mark an accurate stitching line as shown in diagram 1. Repeat on three more white rectangles.

diagram 1

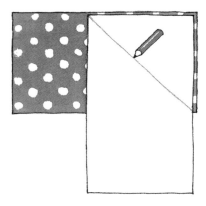

NOTE

Always mark the diagonal in the same direction on the lighter fabric so the blades rotate in the same direction. Left-handers will find it easier to mark from top right to bottom left, and so the blades will rotate clockwise.

2 Place the four marked white rectangles on four print 2 x 3½ in/5.5 x 8.75 cm rectangles at right angles, right sides together, and stitch on marked line. Trim the corners ¼ in/0.75 cm from the stitched line (diagram 2). Open out and finger-press towards the darker fabric.

diagram 2

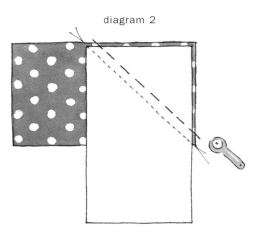

3 Lay out a white background 2 x 5 in/5.5 x 13.5 cm rectangle, a pieced strip, and a print 2 x 5 in/5.5 x 13.5 cm rectangle in the order shown in diagram 3 and stitch together with an accurate ¼ in/0.75 cm seam.

diagram 3

4 Make four of these units for each block and stitch together as shown in diagram 4. Make a total of 30 blocks. Press the blocks.

diagram 4

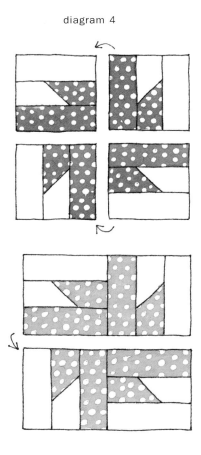

5 Following the quilt assembly diagram on page 120, stitch five blocks together to form a row, then stitch the six rows together to complete the pieced top.

6 From the leftover print fabric, cut strips $3^{1}/_{2}$ in/9.5 cm wide and varying the length from $1^{1}/_{2}$ to 3 in/4 to 8 cm. Stitch enough strips together to make two borders measuring $3^{1}/_{2}$ x $45^{1}/_{2}$ in/9.5 x 129 cm and stitch to the top and bottom of the pieced top. Press lightly.

Finishing

1 Spread the backing right side down on a flat surface, then smooth out the wadding and the patchwork top, right side up, on top. Fasten together with safety pins or baste in a grid.

2 Quilt by hand or machine. Quilt from the centre of the block along the horizontal and vertical seams, returning to the centre each time by a curved arc. Quilt in the same way along the diagonals. Trim the excess wadding and backing level with the pieced top.

3 Join the binding strips with diagonal seams to make a continuous length to fit all round the quilt and use to bind the edges with a double-fold binding, mitred at the corners.

Floral Garland Quilt

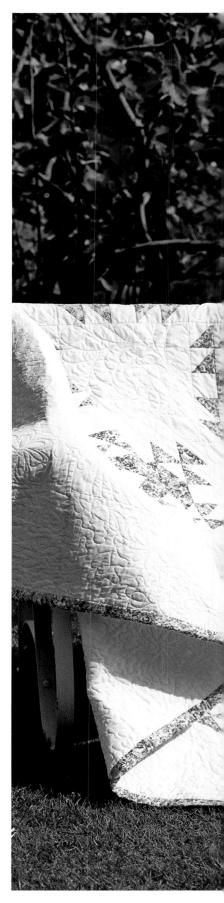

DESIGNED
BY
Katharine
Guerrier

Combine five dainty floral prints with a white-on-white for a delicate quilt to decorate a summer bedroom. The illusion that the blocks are floating is achieved by using the same fabric in the block backgrounds as for the alternate setting blocks and borders. This quilt was quilted on a long-arm quilting machine by Beryl Cadman.

Quilt assembly diagram

Finished size: 87 x 73 in/204 x 167 cm

Materials

All fabrics used in the quilt top are 45 in/115 cm wide, 100% cotton

White: 5$\frac{1}{2}$ yds/5 m

Floral prints: five soft pastel floral prints, 12 in/30 cm of each

Pencil marker

Wadding: 2 oz or low loft, 93 x 79 in/219 x 182 cm

Backing: cotton, 93 x 79 in/219 x 182 cm

Machine quilting thread

Binding: 1 yd/90 cm extra of one of the floral fabrics

Alternative colour schemes

1 Batiks come in a wide variety of rich colours and designs and will give this quilt pattern a contemporary appeal.

2 Red and white has been a favourite combination since the nineteenth century and its popularity still endures.

3 In this Amish-inspired combination, a third colour has been introduced into the centre of the block.

4 A reproduction thirties print is combined with a plain green background to give a vintage look to the block.

Cutting

The white fabric for the borders, edge and corner triangles and squares is cut at this stage. The remaining fabrics are cut as the blocks are stitched.

1 From the white fabric, cut four strips, $8\frac{1}{2}$ x 74 in/ 22 x 189 cm, down the length of the fabric for the borders.

2 Cut three squares, $15\frac{3}{4}$ in/40 cm; cross-cut these across both diagonals to make 12 side triangles. Use one of these as a template to cut two more triangles to make a total of 14 triangles.

3 Cut two 8 in/20.5 cm squares; cut these across one diagonal to make four corner triangles.

4 Cut 12, $10\frac{1}{2}$ in/26.5 cm squares for the alternate setting blocks.

Stitching

Make the blocks four at a time using one of the floral prints combined with the white for each set of four.

1 Cutting across the width of the fabric, cut three strips, $2\frac{7}{8}$ in/7.5 cm deep, and one strip, $2\frac{1}{2}$ in/6.5 cm deep, from one of the floral fabrics and the same from the white fabric.

2 Place one floral and one white $2\frac{7}{8}$ in/7.5 cm strip right sides together. On the wrong side of the white strip, mark off $2\frac{7}{8}$ in/7.5 cm squares, then draw a continuous zigzag line from corner to corner of the marked squares along the length of the strip. Stitch both sides of this line $\frac{1}{4}$ in/0.75 cm away. This can be done in a continuous line, using a $\frac{1}{4}$ in/0.75 cm foot on your sewing machine. If you do not have this facility, mark the sewing line before stitching (diagram 1).

diagram 1

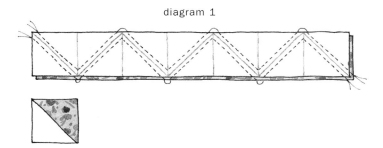

3 Cut on the vertical and diagonal lines. Repeat with the second set of strips (one floral and one white), then cut a 12 in/30.5 cm section from each of the remaining two $2\frac{7}{8}$ in/7.5 cm strips and mark out four more squares. Stitch and cut as before. Press the resulting triangle units open (64 altogether).

4 Take what remains of the third set of $2\frac{7}{8}$ in/7.5 cm strips and cut the width down to $2\frac{1}{2}$ in/6.5 cm. Cut a 21 in/53.5 cm length from both the floral and the white strips. Stitch these together along one long side. Press the seam, then cross-cut into eight $2\frac{1}{2}$ in/6.5 cm segments to make the shorter square units (diagram 2).

diagram 2

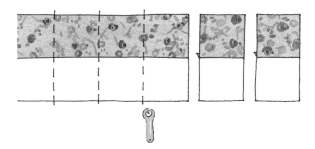

5 To make the longer square units, cut three 11 in/ 28 cm long strips, $2\frac{1}{2}$ in /6.5 cm deep, from the remaining white strip and two 11 in/28 cm long strips from the remaining floral strip. Stitch these strips together along the long sides, taking the usual seam allowance, in the sequence: white/floral/white/floral/white. Press the seams towards the darker fabric, then cross cut into four $2\frac{1}{2}$ in/6.5 cm segments (diagram 3).

diagram 3

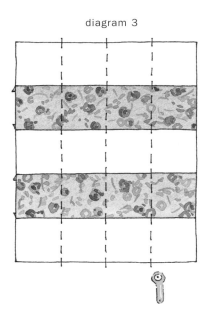

6 Using four of the triangle units made in step 3, make four corner sections for each block, 16 altogether (diagram 4).

diagram 4

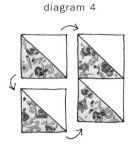

7 To complete the blocks, arrange the block sections in the correct order as shown in diagram 5 and stitch together.

diagram 5

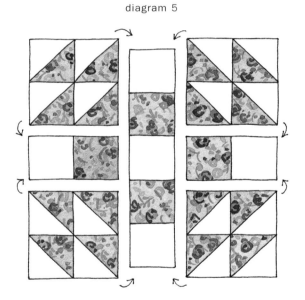

8 Repeat this process with the remaining four floral fabrics to make 20 blocks altogether.

9 Press the pieced blocks thoroughly and, if necessary, adjust the size of the alternate blocks to fit the pieced blocks.

10 Following diagram 6, arrange and stitch the pieced blocks alternately with the plain squares in diagonal rows, adding the corner and side triangles as you work.

11 Press the seams, then stitch the rows together, matching the seams as you work.

diagram 6

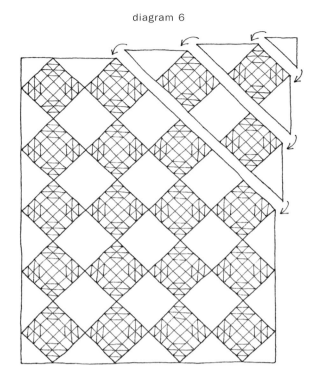

Adding the borders

1 Measure the pieced top through the centre from top to bottom, then trim two of the white border strips to this measurement. Stitch to the sides of the quilt.

2 Measure the pieced top through the centre from side to side, then trim the remaining two white border strips to this measurement. Stitch to the top and bottom.

Finishing

1 If you plan to do your own quilting, spread the backing right side down on a flat surface, then smooth the wadding and the quilt top, right sides up on top. Fasten together with safety pins or baste in a grid.

2 Using the free motion quilting method, quilt over the surface of the quilt in machine quilting thread.

3 Using the extra floral fabric, cut eight strips, $3^{1}/_{2}$ in/9 cm deep, for the binding.

4 Join the binding strips with diagonal seams to make a continuous length to fit all round the quilt and use to bind the edges with a double-fold binding, mitred at the corners.

Citrus Blast Bed Quilt

DESIGNED BY

Nikki Foley

This quilt could be made from a collection of fat quarters; it's also a great way to use up any bright fabrics in unusual shades. The bright citrus colours – lime green, yellow, orange together with red and a blast of purple – will bring sunshine and cheer to any room.

Quilt assembly diagram

Finished quilt size: 88 x 72 in/220 x 180 cm

Materials

All fabrics used in the quilt top are 45 in/115 cm wide, 100% cotton

Citrus green: 1½ yds/1.25 m
Citrus yellow: 1½ yds/1.25 m

Pink/purple: 2⅓ yds/2 m
Orange: 30 in/75 cm
Binding: red, 18 in/45 cm
Backing: 92 x 76 in/230 x 190 cm
Wadding: 92 x 76 in/230 x 190 cm
Machine quilting thread

Alternative colour schemes

1 Shades of pink combined with white are restful.

2 Blues and white are always cool, crisp and clean.

3 A softer colour scheme with stars would suit a child's room.

4 Black, yellow and red will make a really bold quilt.

Cutting

1 From both the citrus green and yellow fabrics, cut ten strips, $4\frac{1}{2}$ in/11.5 cm deep, across the width of the fabric. Cross-cut these into $4\frac{1}{2}$ in/11.5 cm squares. You will need 80 of each colour.

2 From the pink/purple fabric, cut 16 strips, $4\frac{1}{2}$ in/11.5 cm deep, across the width of the fabric. Cross-cut these into rectangles $8\frac{1}{2}$ in/21.5 cm wide. You will need 80 of these.

3 From the orange fabric, cut seven strips, 4 in/10 cm deep, across the width of the fabric for the borders.

4 From the red binding fabric, cut eight strips, 2 in/5 cm deep, across the width of the fabric.

NOTE

If using fat quarters, jumble up all the green squares and put randomly into a pile. Do the same with the yellow squares.

Stitching

1 Place a green and a yellow square right sides together and stitch down one side, taking a $\frac{1}{4}$ in/ 0.75 cm seam allowance. Chain piece the other 79 green and yellow squares together in the same way. Cut apart, press all the seams towards the darker fabric and place in a pile all facing the same way up with the green on the right-hand side.

2 Place one purple rectangle right sides together with one of these two-colour units. Stitch together down one long side, taking the usual seam allowance (diagram 1). Chain piece the units together in the same way. You now have 80 blocks. Press the seams towards the purple.

diagram 1

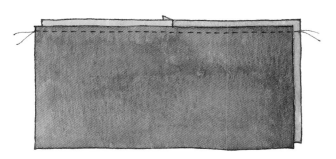

3 Stitch eight blocks together in a row, taking the usual seam allowance and alternating the blocks, so that the purple side runs first across the top, then across the bottom of the block (diagram 2). Press the seams. Repeat to stitch ten rows, all with a purple rectangle in the top left-hand corner.

diagram 2

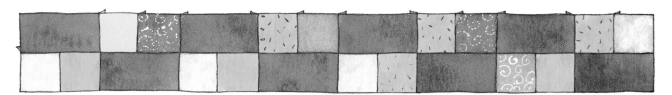

4 Stitch the rows together and press the seams.

Adding the borders

1 Join the seven 4 in/10 cm orange border strips together into one length with diagonal seams.

2 Measure the pieced top through the centre from side to side, then cut two strips to this length from the border strip. Stitch to the top and bottom of the quilt.

3 Measure the pieced top through the centre from top to bottom, then cut two strips to this length from the remaining border strip. Stitch to the sides. Press lightly.

Finishing

1 Spread the backing right side down on a flat surface, then smooth out the wadding and the patchwork top, right side up, on top. Fasten together with safety pins or baste in a grid.

2 Quilt in zigzag lines from the mid point of each block as shown in the photograph. Trim the excess wadding and backing level with the pieced top.

3 Join the binding strips to make a continuous length to fit all round the quilt and use to bind the edges with a double-fold binding, mitred at the corners.

Spring at Last

DESIGNED
BY
Susie Green

This cheerful quilt of horizontal stripes is so simple it can be pieced in a day – the only delay being the decisions on the colour arrangement. It's a perfect opportunity for showcasing those vintage fabrics you have been hiding in your stash. The quilt is an ideal size for a single bed but also lovely for the conservatory or garden bench.

Quilt assembly diagram

Finished size: 75 x 106 in/180 x 245 cm

Materials

All fabrics in the quilt are 100% cotton. Some are 45 in/115 cm, others are recycled fabrics

Body of quilt and outer border: a selection of fabrics totalling 6 yds/5.25 m (this is an approximate figure, as I used some recycled fabrics)

Inner border: 1 yd/90 cm of one colour/print

Backing: $4^{1}/_{2}$ yds/4 m of 60 in/153 cm or $6^{1}/_{4}$ yds/5.2 m of 44 in/115 cm wide

Wadding: Hobbs 100% Organic with Scrim (pre-packed size of 90 x 108 in/230 x 275 cm). This is wonderful wadding that stays put where you want it

Binding: coordinating colour/print, 22 in/55 cm

Alternative colour schemes

1 For children, novelty fabrics are always a hit.

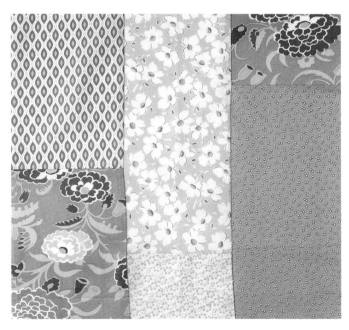

2 Pink and grey has an elegant, stylish quality.

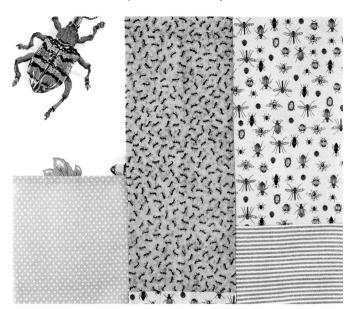

3 Pea green and creams make a quilt that feels fresh and is easy to place, while not necessarily seasonal.

4 Autumnal, earthy, soft colours of sand and aubergine create a lovely winter feeling.

Cutting

1 Cut all of the fabrics for the top, except the inner border and binding, into rectangles, $6^1/_2$ x 20 in/ 16.5 x 50 cm. You need approximately 60 rectangles in total.

2 From the inner border fabric, cut six strips, $4^1/_2$ in/11.5 cm deep, across the width of the fabric.

3 From the binding fabric, cut nine strips, $2^1/_4$ in/ 5.5 cm deep, across the width of the fabric.

4 If using 60 in/153 cm wide backing fabric, cut two lengths of 77 in/196 cm. If using 44 in/115 cm wide backing, cut two lengths of 106 in/270 cm.

5 From the collection of $6^1/_2$ x 20 in/16.5 x 50 cm pieces, cut a few into two, but off-centre (e.g. some pieces will be $6^1/_2$ x 8 in/16.5 x 20 cm and some $6^1/_2$ x 12 in/16.5 x 30 cm). This will help start the staggered look of the strips.

Stitching

1 Place the pieces for the quilt centre into 14 rows, each measuring approximately 60 in/150 cm. The quilt assembly diagram on page 138 shows how the photographed quilt was made up, but your arrangement will depend on your choice of fabrics. Try to arrange the pieces in a brick pattern, so that the vertical seams are staggered (diagram 1). Once you've laid out all of the pieces, step back from the arrangement to make sure you're happy with the colour sequences. Make any adjustments necessary.

diagram 1

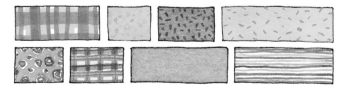

NOTE

Measure 59 in/147 cm from the edge of the table that you are sewing on with a little piece of masking tape. By doing this, you get a rough, quick guide when you have joined enough pieces to make a complete width. Go just beyond the mark and trim later. There's no need to keep measuring. The variety of length makes your quilt interesting. Press all seams in one direction.

2 Stitch the pieces in each row together, then stitch the rows together. Press all the seams in the same direction. Rotary cut the side edges to straighten. (The top at this stage should measure $84^1/_2$ x 54 in/211.5 x 137 cm.)

Adding the borders

1 Join the inner border strips into one long length.

2 Measure the pieced top through the centre from side to side, then cut two strips to this measurement. Stitch to the top and bottom of the pieced top. Press the seams towards the borders.

3 Measure the pieced top through the centre from top to bottom, then cut two strips to this measurement. Stitch to the sides of the pieced top. Press the seams towards the borders.

4 For the outer border, again measure the quilt through the centre from top to bottom. Take some of the remaining 6¹⁄₂ in/16.5 cm pieces and place together into two lengths to this measurement, again checking that you are happy with the colour arrangement. Stitch the pieces together along the short edges, then stitch one pieced strip to the sides of the quilt (diagram 2). Note that the side outer borders are the only place where the strips change direction.

diagram 2

5 Measure the quilt through the centre from side to side, then repeat the arranging and stitching of the remaining 6¹⁄₂ in/16.5 cm pieces to make two more border strips for the top and bottom of the pieced top.

Finishing

NOTE
It's a good idea to unpack the wadding the day before you need it and hang it over the back of a sofa to allow the creases to drop. Alternatively, give the wadding a shake and pop it in a tumble dryer on a cool setting for 10 minutes.

1 Join the backing pieces together to make one piece, 79 x 110 in/190 x 255 cm, taking a ¹⁄₂ in/1.5 cm seam allowance. Press the seam open.

2 Spread the backing right side down on a flat surface, then smooth out the wadding and the pieced top, right side up, on top. Fasten together with safety pins or baste in a grid.

3 Hand or machine quilt. I used a longarm quilting machine to machine quilt in an edge-to-edge pattern.

4 Join all the binding strips into one length and use to bind the quilt with a double-fold binding, mitred at the corners.

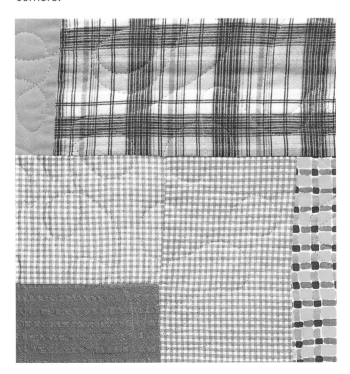

THE CONTRIBUTORS

Nikki Foley has a HNC in interior design and uses this to her advantage when designing quilts and patterns for her business 'The Sewing Shed': www.thesewingshed@aol.com

Susie Green is an experienced designer who runs her own quilting business.

Katharine Guerrier is a leading quilt designer, who frequently exhibits in national shows. She is also the author of a number of books on quilt techniques.

Jean Hunt is an experienced teacher, having taught patchwork for many years in Stroud, Gloucestershire. She is the resident teacher for Abigail Crafts.

Jill Leman specialises in textiles, watercolour painting and book design.

Mary O'Riordan is an experienced quiltmaker who works at The Quilt Room in Dorking, Surrey

Sarah Wellfair is a qualified teacher who runs a full programme of workshops from her patchwork shop, Goose Chase Quilting, at Leckhampton in Gloucestershire.

Rita Whitehorn is an experienced quiltmaker and designer, who makes quilts to commission.

Alison Wood teaches classes and works part-time at The Quilt Room in Dorking, Surrey.

SUPPLIERS

UK

Abigail Crafts
3-5 Regent Street
Stonehouse
Gloucestershire GL10 2AA
Tel: 01453 823691
www.abigailcrafts.co.uk
Patchwork and embroidery supplies

The Bramble Patch
West Street
Weedon
Northants NN7 4QU
Tel: 01327 342212
Patchwork and quilting supplies

Custom Quilting Limited
"Beal na Tra"
Derrymihan West
Castletownbere
Co Cork, Eire
Email: patches@iol.ie
Long arm quilting services

The Cotton Patch
1285 Stratford Road
Hall Green
Birmingham B28 9AJ
Tel: 0121 702 2840
Patchwork and quilting supplies

Creative Quilting
3 Bridge Road
East Molesey
Surrey KT8 9EU
Tel: 020 8941 7075
Specialist retailer

Fred Aldous Ltd
P.O Box 135
37 Lever Street
Manchester M1 1LW
Tel: 0161 236 2477
Mail order craft materials

Goose Chase Quilting
65 Great Norwood Street
Leckhampton
Cheltenham GL50 2BQ
Tel: 01242 512639
Patchwork and quilting supplies

Hab-bits
Unit 9, Vale Business Park
Cowbridge
Vale of Glamorgan
CF71 7PF
Tel: 01446 775150
Haberdashery supplies

Patchwork Direct
c/o Heirs & Graces
King Street
Bakewell
Derbyshire DE45 1DZ
Tel: 01629 815873
www.patchworkdirect.com
Patchwork and quilting supplies

Purely Patchwork
23 High Street
Linlithgow
West Lothian
Scotland
Tel: 01506 846200
Patchwork and quilting supplies

Quilting Solutions
Firethorn
Rattlesden Road
Drinkstone
Bury St Edmunds
Suffolk IP30 9TL
Tel: 01449 735280
Email: firethorn@lineone.net
www.quiltingsolutions.co.uk
Long arm quilting services

Stitch in Time
293 Sandycombe Road
Kew
Surrey TW9 3LU
Tel: 020 8948 8462
www.stitchintimeuk.com
Specialist quilting retailer

Strawberry Fayre
Chagford
Devon TQ13 8EN
Tel: 01647 433250
Mail order fabrics and quilts

Sunflower Fabrics
157-159 Castle Road
Bedford MK40 3RS
Tel: 01234 273819
www.sunflowerfabrics.com
Quilting supplies

The Quilt Loft
9/10 Havercroft Buildings
North Street
Worthing
West Sussex BN11 1DY
Tel: 01903 233771
Quilt supplies, classes and
workshops

The Quilt Room
20 West Street
Dorking
Surrey RH4 1BL
Tel: 01306 740739
www.quiltroom.co.uk
Quilt supplies, classes and
workshops
Mail order: The Quilt Room
c/o Carvilles
Station Road
Dorking
Surrey RH4 1XH
Tel: 01306 877307

The Sewing Shed
Shanahill West
Keel
Castlemaine
Co Kerry, Eire
www.thesewingshed@aol.com
Patchwork and quilting
supplies

Worn and Washed
The Walled Garden
48 East Street
Olney
Bucks MK 46 4DW
Tel: 01234 240881
Email:kim@wornandwashed-
fabrics.com

South Africa

Crafty Supplies
Stadium on Main
Main Road
Claremont 7700
Tel: 021 671 0286

Fern Gully
46 3rd Street
Linden
2195
Tel: 011 782 7941

Stitch 'n' Stuff
140 Lansdowne Road
Claremont 7700
Tel: 021 674 4059

Pied Piper
69 1st Avenue
Newton Park
Port Elizabeth 6001
Tel: 041 365 1616

Quilt Talk
40 Victoria Street
George 6530
Tel: 044 873 2947

Nimble Fingers
Shop 222
Kloof Village Mall
Village Road
Kloof 3610
Tel: 031 764 6283

Quilt Tech
9 Louanna Avenue
Kloofendal
Extension 5 1709
Tel: 011 679 4386

Simply Stitches
2 Topaz Street
Albernarle
Germiston 1401
Tel: 011 902 6997

Quilting Supplies
42 Nellnapius Drive
Irene 0062
Tel: 012 667 2223

Australia

Patchwork Plus
Shop 81
7-15 Jackson Avenue
Miranda
NSW 2228
Tel: (02) 9540 278

Patchwork of Essendon
96 Fletcher Street
Essendon
VIC 3040
Tel: (03) 9372 0793

Quilts and Threads
827 Lower North East Road
Dernancourt
SA 5075
Tel: (08) 8365 6711

Riverlea Cottage Quilts
Shop 4, 330 Unley Road
Hyde Park
SA 5061
Tel: (08) 8373 0653

Country Patchwork Cottage
10/86 Erindale Road
Balcatta
WA 6021
Tel: (08) 9345 3550

The Quilters Store
22 Shaw Street
Auchenflower
QLD 4066
Tel: (07) 3870 0408

New Zealand

Patchwork Barn
132 Hinemoa Street
Birkenhead
Auckland
Tel: (09) 480 5401

Stitch and Craft
32 East Tamaki Road
Papatoetoe
Auckland
Tel: (09) 278 1351
Fax: (09) 278 1356

The Patchwork Shop
356 Grey Street
Hamilton
Tel: (07) 856 6365

The Quilt Shop
35 Pearn Place
Northcote Shopping Centre
Auckland
Tel: (09) 480 0028
Fax: (09) 480 0380

Grandmothers Garden
Patchwork and Quilting
1042 Gordonton Road
Gordonton
Hamilton
Tel: (07) 824 3050

Needlecraft Distributors
600 Main Street
Palmerston North
Tel: (06) 356 4793
Fax: (06) 355 4594

**Hands Ashford Craft Supply
Store**
5 Normans Road
Christchurch
Tel: (03) 355 9099
www.hands.co.nz

Stitches
351 Colombo Street
Christchurch
Tel: (03) 379 1868
Fax: (03) 377 2347
www.stitches.co.nz

Variety Handcrafts
106 Princes Street
Dunedin
Tel: (03) 474 1088

Spotlight Stores
Whangarei (09) 430 7220
Wairau Park (09) 444 0220
Henderson (09) 836 0888
Panmure (09) 527 0915
Manukau City (09) 263 6760
Hamilton (07) 839 1793
Rotorua (07) 343 6901
New Plymouth (06) 757 3575
Gisborne (06) 863 0037
Hastings (06) 878 5223
Palmerston North (06) 357
6833
Porirua (04) 238 4055
Wellington (04) 472 5600
Christchurch (03) 377 6121
Dunedin (03) 477 1478
www.spotlight.net.nz

INDEX